Raeann R. Hamon, PhD, CF [barcode] *Editor*

P9-BIR-608

International Family Studies
Developing Curricula and Teaching Tools

Pre-publication REVIEWS, COMMENTARIES, EVALUATIONS . . .

"This is a useful text for instructors organizing family studies courses that carry an international theme. The editors provide a practical and informative set of readings and offer teaching insights, teaching tools, and teaching techniques to support instructors and instruction. In particular, the book is organized around teaching techniques (electronic portfolios, group presentations), book reviews of books related to teaching international family courses, and a set of feature articles on topics related to such courses (international study experiences, teaching family science at international universities outside the United States). This should be a functional resource for instructors of a variety of international family studies courses."

Stephan M. Wilson, PhD, CLFE
Professor and Chair, Department of Human Development and Family Studies, University of Nevada, Reno

"I am looking forward to having this compilation available for my own use and to share with others. As the communities we live and work in become more diverse, it behooves undergraduate programs of study in family science, social work, sociology, psychology, and nursing to offer at least one course with a focus on international families. This book provides scholarly insight into how such courses can, even should, be designed and delivered so as to bring about student learning and growth. Nearly every aspect of teaching such a course is addressed from rationale and underlying conceptualizations to learning activities, assignments, and travel experiences. Every reader will come upon an idea or approach that can be incorporated into his or her own teaching. I am confident that the result will be rewarding for both teacher and student alike."

Deborah Gentry, EdD
Professor and Associate Dean, College of Applied Science and Technology, Illinois State University

More pre-publication
REVIEWS, COMMENTARIES, EVALUATIONS . . .

"**A** must-read for anyone developing or reinvigorating a course with content on international families. This book provides resources and references, student assignments, in-class activities, and programs for use in the community. Although I have taught a class on family diversity for several years, I found useful tools in this book that I will now incorporate into my class, such as presenting a case study and analyzing it from the perspective of individuals from multiple cultures, using electronic resources, and ways to rethink and restructure group projects/presentations in the classroom."

Suzanne R. Smith, PhD
*Associate Professor, Associate Chair,
and Program Director, Department
of Human Development,
Washington State University, Vancouver*

The Haworth Press
New York • London • Oxford

International Family Studies
Developing Curricula and Teaching Tools

THE HAWORTH PRESS

New, recent, and forthcoming titles of related interest

International Family Studies

Studies

Developing Curricula and Teaching Tools

Raeann R. Hamon, PhD, CFLE
Editor

The Haworth Press
New York • London • Oxford

For more information on this book or to order, visit
http://www.haworthpress.com/store/product.asp?sku=5609

or call 1-800-HAWORTH (800-429-6784) in the United States and Canada
or (607) 722-5857 outside the United States and Canada

or contact orders@HaworthPress.com

Published by

The Haworth Press, Inc., 10 Alice Street, Binghamton, NY 13904-1580.

PUBLISHER'S NOTE
The development, preparation, and publication of this work has been undertaken with great care. However, the Publisher, employees, editors, and agents of The Haworth Press are not responsible for any errors contained herein or for consequences that may ensue from use of materials or information contained in this work. The Haworth Press is committed to the dissemination of ideas and information according to the highest standards of intellectual freedom and the free exchange of ideas. Statements made and opinions expressed in this publication do not necessarily reflect the views of the Publisher, Directors, management, or staff of The Haworth Press, Inc., or an endorsement by them.

Cover design by Jennifer M. Gaska.

Library of Congress Cataloging-in-Publication Data

International family studies : developing curricula and teaching tools / Raeann R. Hamon, editor.
    p. cm.
Includes bibliographical references and index.
ISBN-13: 978-0-7890-2923-2 (hard : alk. paper)
ISBN-10: 0-7890-2923-5 (hard : alk. paper)
ISBN-13: 978-0-7890-2924-9 (soft : alk. paper)
ISBN-10: 0-7890-2924-3 (soft : alk. paper)
    1. Family—Study and teaching. 2. Marriage—Study and teaching. I. Hamon, Raeann R.

HQ10.I52 2005
306.8071—dc22
                                                        2005025971

CONTENTS

ABOUT THE EDITOR

Raeann R. Hamon, PhD, CFLE, is Distinguished Professor of Family Science and Gerontology and Chair of the Department of Human Development and Family Science at Messiah College, Grantham, Pennsylvania. She co-edited *Mate Selection Across Cultures* (with Bron Ingoldsby), served as an associate editor for the *International Encyclopedia of Marriage and Family,* and is currently working on a book titled *Culturally Diverse Families: A Family Science Perspective* (with Bahira Sherif-Trask). A certified family life educator, she is on the board of the Association of Councils and is an active member of the International Section of the National Council on Family Relations. She is involved in cross-cultural research, largely in the Bahamas, publishing and writing on Bahamian folklore and family life.

doi:10.1300/5609_a

CONTRIBUTORS

Sylvia M. Asay, PhD, CFLE, is Associate Professor of family studies at the University of Nebraska at Kearney. Her research focuses on family strengths in postcommunist countries and she teaches courses in marriage and family relationships and cross-cultural family patterns.

Sue Bailey, PhD, serves as Professor and Director of the School of Human Ecology at Tennessee Technological University in Cookeville, Tennessee. She holds the CFCS (certification in family and consumer sciences) from the American Association of Family and Consumer Sciences. Dr. Bailey teaches professional development courses and works extensively with student organizations in family and consumer sciences. She holds service grants that train child care providers and a research grant to study childhood nutrition. She has been a presenter at the International Federation of Home Economics conference.

Mozhdeh B. Bruss, PhD, MPH, RD, is the Deither H. Haenicke Center Scholar for International and Area Studies, and Assistant Professor in Family and Consumer Sciences at Western Michigan University. She teaches undergraduate and graduate courses in nutrition as it relates to culture, community, family, and gender. Dr. Bruss has extensive experience with community education programs in the United States, West Indies, Pacific Islands, China, and Latin America. Currently, she is principal investigator for the Childhood Obesity Prevention Research Project, which is developing a scientifically based and culturally sensitive intervention curriculum for primary caregivers targeting the prevention of childhood obesity.

Eileen Buckley, BS, is a faculty specialist in family and consumer sciences at Western Michigan University. She teaches undergraduate and graduate courses in teacher education for career and technical education. Ms. Buckley has extensive experience with teaching. Her passions lie in instructing new teachers to realize that every student deserves to be able to learn to the best of his or her ability and it is

doi:10.1300/5609_b

their duty to establish methods and procedures that will allow this to occur. The key to this awareness is to know about and empathize with world community members that share this planet.

María E. Canabal, PhD, is Professor, Department of Family and Consumer Sciences at Illinois State University–Normal, where she teaches undergraduate and graduate courses in family/consumer economics and family resource management. Her research topics include work and family, female-headed families, marital dissolution, cohabitation and marital stability, minority issues in education and housing, women power and fertility decisions, college student's labor force participation, poverty issues, premarital pregnancy, and others. The results of the research on these topics have been presented in national and international conferences. She received a Fulbright fellowship in 1995, assigned to Avinashilingham University in South India.

Ann Creighton-Zollar, PhD, CFLE, is Associate Professor of Sociology at Virginia Commonwealth University. She teaches both undergraduate- and graduate-level family courses. Her work on this book grew out of her participation in a Preparing Tomorrow's Teachers to Use Technology grant.

Carol Anderson Darling, PhD, CFLE, is Margaret Sandels Professor of Human Sciences and a distinguished teaching professor at Florida State University, where she teaches both undergraduate and graduate courses in the Department of Family and Child Sciences. She is the past president of the National Council on Family Relations. Twice she has been a Fulbright scholar in teaching and research at the University of Helsinki and is currently Docent in Family and consumer Sciences at the University of Helsinki. She has also taught and given educational presentations in various locations in Finland, Costa Rica, Taiwan, and South Korea.

Shi-Ruei Sherry Fang, PhD, is Associate Professor in Family and Child Studies at Northern Illinois University. She is originally from Taiwan. Her research interests include parenting and child rearing in different cultures, as well as in immigrant families.

Cherie K. Fernsler, BA, is from Cleona, Pennsylvania. She graduated in 2005 with a bachelor's degree in human development and family science from Messiah College.

Lamont A. Flowers, PhD, is the Distinguished Professor of Educational Leadership in the Department of Leadership, Counselor

Education, Human and Organizational Development and Director of the Charles H. Houston Center for the Study of the Black Experience in Education in the Eugene T. Moore School of Education at Clemson University.

Barbara J. Frazier, PhD, is Associate Professor in the Department of Family and Consumer Sciences at Western Michigan University, where she teaches courses in entrepreneurship and retailing. Her research interests are focused on entrepreneurship in rural environments. Her current work involves developing a model to predict entrepreneurial intention in a range of subpopulations.

Lisa A. Guion, EdD, is currently Associate Professor in the Department of Family, Youth, and Community Sciences, Institute of Food and Agricultural Sciences (IFAS), at the University of Florida. She teaches courses in program planning and evaluation, as well as cultural diversity and awareness. She is the author of several journal articles related to designing culturally relevant educational programs and developing culturally competent educators. She is also a contributor to a case study in *Diversity Issues in American Colleges and Universities: Case Studies for Higher Education and Student Affairs Professionals.*

Christina Holland, MA candidate, is a marriage and family therapist for Monty L. Meier, PhD, & Associates, Olympia and Aberdeen, Washington. She specializes in treating individuals, couples, families, and children. She is a member of both national and state organizations and attends monthly postgraduate meetings. Christina has been honored by The American Association for Marriage and Family Therapy with a national fellowship and was awarded Student of the Year 2004 by the Washington Association for Marriage and Family Therapy. She has authored and co-authored four national publications and remains dedicated to continuing education in her field.

Stacy N. Howard, MS, CFLE, received her BS in Sociology from the University of Louisville and MS in Family Relations from Florida State University, where she is currently a doctoral candidate. She is director of research for a state-level nonprofit organization working to serve families with young children. Stacy is an award-winning teaching assistant and is a recognized trainer in the field of early care and education in Florida.

Bron B. Ingoldsby, PhD, now deceased, was Associate Professor in the School of Family Life at Brigham Young University, Salt Lake

City, Utah. A leader in the area of cross-cultural family research, he was the author of numerous professional publications including (with Suzanna Smith) *Families in Multicultural Perspective* and (with Raeann Hamon) *Mate Selection Across Cultures*. His most recent work focused on family change among the Hutterian Brethren and marriage in Latin American. He was honored as the 2002 recipient of the Jan Trost Award for Outstanding Contributions to Comparative Family Studies by the National Council on Family Relations.

Teresa McDowell, EdD, is Director, Marriage and Family Therapy, in the School of Family Studies at the University of Connecticut. Her professional interests and publications include an emphasis on critical multicultural research, social justice in family therapy, and cultural democracy in family therapy training and supervision.

Tami James Moore, PhD, CFLE, is Associate Professor of Family Studies at the University of Nebraska at Kearney. Her areas of special interest include diversity development and human sexual behavior.

Sylvia Niehuis, PhD, is Assistant Professor in the Department of Family, Consumer, and Human Development at Utah State University, where she teaches courses in marriage and family relationships, family and cultural diversity, dating and courtship, research methods, and family theories. Her research interests are focused on dating, courtship, and the transition to marriage.

Paul L. Schvaneveldt, PhD, CFLE, is Assistant Professor in the Department of Child and Family Studies at Weber State University, Ogden, Utah. His research focuses on families and adolescents in Latin America. Specifically, he has studied adolescent social competency in Bolivia, Ecuador, and Chile, family dynamics and at-risk behaviors of adolescents in Ecuador, and mate selection practices and preferences in Ecuador and Bolivia.

Anita M. Subramaniam, PhD, completed her PhD from Ohio State University in Consumer Science and was the program coordinator and faculty of Consumer Affairs at Montclair State University until 2004. She returned to India for family reasons in 2005 and has been in the corporate training division of Cognizant Technology Solutions Inc. She pursues research on training, advises on pedagogy, and reviews training methodology at the Cognizant Academy.

Melinda K. Swafford, PhD, received her doctorate in Exceptional Learning: Young Children and Families from Tennessee Technological University. She is currently employed in the School of Human Ecology at Tennessee Technological University. She currently teaches the content area of child development and family relations, children with exceptionalities and family and consumer sciences education.

Rebekah A. Thomas, PhD, received her doctorate in Exceptional Learning: Applied Behavior and Learning from Tennessee Technological University. She is currently a behavior analyst with the Columbus Organization and provides behavioral services for adults and children with mental retardation and developmental disabilities. Rebekah is also adjunct faculty at Tennessee Technological University where she teaches undergraduate- and graduate-level courses related to positive behavior supports and special education.

Steven K. Wisensale, PhD, is Professor of Public Policy in the School of Family Studies at the University of Connecticut where he received the Excellence in Teaching Award. He teaches courses in family policy, comparative family policy, family law, and aging policy. His research interests include work and family issues and aging policy. His book, *Family Leave Policy: The Political Economy of Work and Family in America* was published by M.E. Sharpe in 2001. He is the recipient of two Fulbright fellowships and is a senior scholar and board member at the Council of Contemporary Families. He is also the former chair of the family policy section of the National Council on Family Relations.

Maha N. Younes, PhD, ACSW, LCSW, LMHP, is Social Work Professor and Program Director at the University of Nebraska at Kearney. Her teaching focus is on social policy and clinical mental health practice and her research interests include children, family, and cultural competence.

Preface

During 2004, the United Nations' Tenth Anniversary of the International Year of the Family (IYF) gave rise to a renewed impetus to strengthen and support families around the globe. For me and many of my colleagues in family science, the International Year of the Family gave us pause to consider ways in which to better understand and integrate information about families and their experiences from around the world on our own campuses and in our family science programs. As educators, we recognize our responsibility to adequately prepare future family professionals for cross-cultural competence, and greater global awareness and understanding.

The authors in this book responded to a call for proposals for a special, guest-edited issue of the *Journal of Teaching in Marriage and Family* in which they were asked to submit manuscripts that focus on teaching about international families. Even though Haworth discontinued publishing the journal, there was great interest in and commitment to producing a book on this topic. Thus, this book contains chapters which delineate innovative pedagogical strategies and methods which better prepare our students for working with diverse families.

Thus, *International Family Studies: Developing Curricula and Teaching Tools* is a collection of ideas and resources for faculty members who wish to enhance the international content of their marriage and family curricula and experience of their family science students and faculty. The book begins with a chapter co-authored by Fang, McDowell, and Holland, who help us to consider strategies for internationalizing family science programs. In their chapter, "Internationalizing Family Science Programs: A Spherical Expansion of Inclusive Perspectives," they set the stage for a transformative, systemic commitment to diversity. They delineate the importance of: faculty engagement and development, teaching practices and curriculum, and the student body to internationalization efforts, offering specific examples and recommendations within each category. In "Cultural

doi:10.1300/5609_c

Lessons in Sexuality: Comparison of Parent-Child Communication Styles in Three Cultures," Darling and Howard offer an engaging classroom exercise, a circular role-play method for addressing parent-child communication about sexuality. The results of the data they collected suggest that this activity increases cultural understanding among participants. In "How Big is the Penguin? Designing and Teaching a Course in Comparative Family Policy," Wisensale explores course objectives, content, class exercises, learning materials, projects, and grading criteria for a comparative family policy course. Recognizing that many of our programs include extension or outreach activities, authors Guion and Flowers in "Breaking Down Cultural Barriers" report the planning, implementation, and evaluation of Strengthening Programs to Reach Diverse Audiences, a curriculum designed to enhance the cultural competence of educators who need to work more effectively with children, youths and families from diverse backgrounds.

Chapters 5 through 8 expand our traditional classrooms, either psychologically or physically, placing us in locations around the world. Asay, Younes, and Moore, in "The Cultural Transformation Model: Promoting Cultural Competence Through International Study Experiences," review and evaluate the impact of international study groups on cultural perspectives of students. They also propose a Cultural Transformation Model to demonstrate the process many students encounter when engaged in a cross-cultural study tour.

In "Global Ecology Instructional Model: An Application for the Study of Families in an International Context," Bruss, Frazier, and Buckley outline a model intended to function as a guide for developing courses that encourage an ecological approach to the study of families in countries around the world. They incorporate a series of activities (e.g., self-assessment, case study analysis, country-based research) that foster cultural literacy and competence among students.

In her chapter, Canabal endorses "The Fulbright Programs Model for Teaching and Learning About International Families," as well as offers useful feedback from participants in the programs. In an effort to enlarge our exposure to family science programs around the world, Schvaneveldt and Ingoldsby offer "Teaching Family Science in Ecuador." Their experience with the University of Casa Grande might encourage others to partner with family programs abroad in a variety of mutually beneficial research and learning activities.

In Part II of the book, "Teaching Tools and Techniques," Niehuis shares how she creatively employs student group presentations to increase student knowledge about different ethnic and cultural groups. Swafford, Thomas, and Bailey review an innovative, bilingual Affirmation Book Project, which was incorporated into a Head Start program and describe its effectiveness in affirming individual children, promoting literacy skills, and creating a climate of multicultural understanding. In "Creating an Electronic Portfolio to Integrate Multiculturalism in Teaching Family Economics," Subramaniam describes a fascinating project in which she requires her students to use electronic media in gathering cultural, political, economic, lifestyle, religious, and traditions information about countries different from their own.

Continuing this section is Creighton-Zollar's "Communicating Across Preferences: A Comparative Family Systems Example." The author describes how students, after they identify their own learning styles using the VARK Web site, select two family systems for comparative analysis on nine variables using eHRAF. Student-run work groups then make multisensory presentations of their findings.

Faculty who wish to develop study-abroad courses as part of the family science or general education curriculum will benefit from Hamon and Fernsler's chapter called, "Using Cross-Cultural Study Courses to Teach About International Families." The authors offer a thorough delineation of the logistics of offering such a course and provide an example of a Bahamaian cross-cultural course that is co-led by Hamon.

My hope is that this book will serve as a springboard for your own creative activity relative to internationalizing your family science curricula. I would like to express my appreciation to the following reviewers for sharing their time and talent in the creation of this project:

John Addleman   Steve Brown
Neetu Arora   Molly Burke
Mayra Bamaca   Lynda Cable
Karin Bartoszuk   Joyce Chang
Debra Berke   Barbara Clauss
Mary Bold   Ann Creighton-Zollar
David Briscoe   Annamaria Csizmadia

Maya David
Dan Detzner
Denise Donnelly
Pam Ellwanger
Gul Erden
Robert Flynn Corwyn
Tammy Harpel
Mark Heyward
Jeanne Hilton
Nuran Hortacsu
Abraham Hwang
Bron Ingoldsby
Arminta Jacobson
Greg Janson
Edward Kain
Janice Kelly
Kirti Kanitkar
Yesim Korkut
Vera Maass
Ramona Marotz-Baden

Nilufer Medora
Chloe Merrill
Frances Murphy
Marie Radina
Deborale Richardson-Bouie
William Rose
Richard Sale
Marie Saracino
Walter Schumm
Paul Schvaneveldt
Rudy Seward
Bahira Sherif Trask
Lauren Smith
Anne Stanberry
Penny Stoddard
Richard Tuveson
Barbara Vinick
Denese Vlosky
Monte Wainscott
Yan Ruth Xia

PART I: INTERNATIONALIZING THE CURRICULUM

Chapter 1

Internationalizing Family Science Programs: A Spherical Expansion of Inclusive Perspectives

Shi-Ruei Sherry Fang
Teresa McDowell
Christina Holland

Most educators agree on the importance of internationalizing higher education in the twenty-first century. The internationalization of universities in the United States increases the political significance of assembling a diverse student body. In the post-September 11 era, it serves the function of enhancing national security, economic development, cross-cultural understanding, and the forming of a national identity in today's global society. Most important, internationalization provides an opportunity to fulfill basic missions of universities: to develop cross-cultural awareness, which in turn, provides a forum for learning, research, and social debates. More than half a million students from other countries currently study in the United States, and international students account for 12 percent of graduate enroll-

© 2006 by The Haworth Press, Inc. All rights reserved.
doi:10.1300/5609_01

ments (Altbach, 2002). Universities must become more responsive to the needs of international learners. Specific to family science programs, international concerns need to become integral in preparing all students to work in an increasingly interdependent world. With these imperatives in mind we considered internationalizing family science education.

Internationalizing family science programs is a formidable task that begins by including global concerns in our educational agendas and inspecting our pedagogies from international perspectives. As educators, we must carefully consider the nature and direction of our efforts to ensure that we act in globally responsible ways. In an era in which economic globalization is further advantaging countries of the northern hemisphere (e.g., North America, Europe, Pacific Rim) over countries of the southern hemisphere (most others) it is important that we do not engage in education that inadvertently contributes to international inequity. Yang (2002) argued, "for a university, internationalization means the awareness and operation of interactions within and between cultures through its teaching, research and service functions, with the ultimate aim of achieving mutual understanding across cultural borders" (p. 83). Yang's definition reflects the overlap between efforts to emphasize multiculturalism and efforts to internationalize family science programs. Internationalism, therefore, refers to a multitude of activities aimed at providing an educational experience that emphasizes cultural integration. Both multiculturalism and internationalism require sensitivity to diversity, inclusion, and equity. We approach international concerns recognizing that multiculturalism is an integral part of this effort. Internationalizing family science programs requires us to critique prevailing Euro-American centered theoretical assumptions; to go beyond an exclusive focus on U.S. families; and to investigate how our educational practices privilege some while marginalizing others. We believe family science programs should strive to:

1. develop cultures of pluralism in which multiple perspectives are cultivated and valued;
2. support the education and equal opportunity of international students;
3. enhance the relevance of international experience for all students;

4. encourage respect and connection across national boundaries;
5. promote the ongoing process of cultural self-awareness; and
6. consider systems of privilege and oppression to enhance the ability of all of us to support family life within a social context.

In this chapter we suggest that family science faculty consider numerous areas to begin internationalizing their programs. First, we look at the university system in finding ways to support all students, including international students. Second, we consider how to promote internationally engaged faculty. Third, we offer reasons for promoting international family science research. Fourth, we consider teaching practices and curriculum. Finally, we discuss recruiting and supporting an internationally diverse student body. We offer examples from our work that we have found helpful in our own journeys toward internationalization.

As authors, we wrote this chapter from three different cultural perspectives. We saw this as beneficial, offering us a polyocular view of internationalizing family science education. The first author, Shi-Ruei Sherry Fang, is Chinese American and emigrated to the United States from Taiwan as an international student herself. She then became a faculty member in a family science program. The second author, Teresa McDowell, is European American, was a stay-at-home student, and has taught in two marriage and family therapy (MFT) graduate programs. The third author, Christina Holland, is Vietnam-ese-European American and all of her education has been in the United States. She is currently a graduate student in a MFT program. All of us have recent experience with international students: the third author as a student/colleague, the first and second authors as faculty.

EDUCATIONAL INSTITUTIONS AND FAMILY STUDIES PROGRAMS

Although the rhetoric of educators has captured the significance of internationalization of higher education, there is little agreement as to what this means or how it can be implemented (Dilys, 2000). Furthermore, even with the increased awareness of the importance of including international perspectives in higher education, institutions are slow in responding to this need. Educational institutions in the United

States are often sites where deeply embedded, Euro-American, middle-class, male ideologies are reflected (Gloria & Pope-Davis, 1998), exclusion and marginalization routinely occur (Ridley & Thompson, 1999), and diversity is not affirmed (Vazquez, 1998). Institutional concerns include culturally biased admission policies, low rates of faculty of color and/or international faculty representation, minimal support for international students and students of color, and culturally exclusive learning environments and curricula. As pointed out by Hayward (1995), "Part of American higher education is to go beyond a Eurocentric view of international education and to recognize the variety of ways in which Africa, Asia, Latin America, and the Middle East are important to our future success stories, challenges, and opportunities" (p. 119). An institution that is truly committed to internationalizing education should have a comprehensive, multifaceted, coherent program of action that integrates broad international perspectives into all aspects of education. This begins with a clear set of specific policies and initiatives that relate to recruitment of international students, collaboration with academic institutions in other countries, transformation of curriculum content beyond a U.S. and Western European focus, and a mission statement that clearly delineates the inclusion of global awareness and cultural competencies to students' learning outcomes. Given the current political and economic climate, internationalization needs to remain a primary and central goal of academe.

Varying degrees of social awareness, sensitivity, and commitment for change exist in the larger academy. This may be reflected in the amount of energy, resources, and enthusiasm each brings to the table for the internationalization effort. The bureaucracy of academic institutions presents tremendous barriers to the type of flexibility that may be necessary to internationalize a discipline. Changing organizational policies and procedures requires shifts in the attitudes, beliefs, assumptions, and norms embedded in the academic culture in which family science programs are situated.

Family science programs are not without problems either. They often pay little attention to non-Western works and practices, demonstrating an intrinsic assumption that one particular tradition and worldview is superior. Today, information and ideas flow at lightening speed, and communities and workplaces reflect a growing diversity of cultures, languages, attitudes, and values. Family science programs must situate children and family issues in a global context by adopting a comparative perspective and exposing students to complex international issues. Paige and Williams (2001) recently surveyed undergraduate students from a college of Family and Consumer Sciences. They discovered that the overwhelming majority of students sampled recognized the importance of international understanding to their professional development. However, most of them felt they did not learn much about other cultures from the coursework.

International education and social awareness need to be integrated throughout family science programs. Readings, exercises, and course requirements relating international perspectives should be folded into all coursework. There needs to be open dialogue about how the narrowly focused Euro-American-centered theories and methods exclude the positions of other cultures. We need to carefully critique, from a pluralistic viewpoint, the traditional Western model that has permeated family science training in order to create space for a truly respectful, plural learning environment that both welcomes and challenges students of all backgrounds.

FACULTY ENGAGEMENT AND DEVELOPMENT

To successfully attract and retain quality international students and to promote international learning for all students, it is essential to build and maintain an academic, social, and cultural climate that values diversity within the academic community. This includes an institutionalized commitment to provide sufficient funding, strong executive leadership, a supportive structure, and human resources to meet these goals (McDowell, Fang, Brownlee, Gomez Young & Khanna, 2002). As noted by McNairy (1996), having more culturally diverse students, although essential, does not result in an automatic reduction of prejudice and stereotypes, nor does it automatically increase tolerance and awareness of other cultures. An internationalized discipline requires more than bringing students together and/or offering a series of courses that promote international learning. There must be a commitment from the entire campus to create a learning environment that fosters the goal of internationalization. Among various factors, faculty engagement and development are vital to internationalization efforts.

CASE EXAMPLE: DEVELOPING FACULTY MULTICULTURAL COMPETENCE

The Multicultural Curriculum Transformation Institute at Northern Illinois University exemplifies an institutional commitment to faculty development. The provost's office initiated and funded the institute in order to achieve a curriculum and campus environment that is more receptive to domestic and international cultural differences. The primary goal of the institute depends upon the willingness of the faculty to undertake the redesign of an instructional course, integrating multicultural pedagogy and scholarship.

Typically, the seven-day workshop has provided faculty members with an opportunity to engage in intense learning in the science of teaching as well as relevant content issues. The faculty has implemented a redesigned curriculum in the subsequent academic year. Furthermore, they have presented a summary of the redesigned curriculum to the university. A stipend is associated with this effort. The completion of the institute is linked to the university merit system. Since its inception in 1993, the institute has supported over 120 tenure-track faculty members. In 2003, due to the success of the institute, the scope was expanded to include nonfaculty teaching staff. Although it is not designed specifically for the family science faculty, the institute is a step toward the development of a more multicultural community for all students. Funding to support the infusion of international content to existing courses or to develop new ones with international focus are modest investments in curricular improvement.

Aside from curriculum redesign, other faculty development efforts are also vital to the internationalization process. One of the more effective ways for faculty to develop a sense of commitment to internationalization is through supporting faculty travel abroad. This is especially important for family science faculty. Not only does this allow faculty to observe native family life and child rearing in the natural cultural, social, and political settings of other countries, but also provides faculty the opportunity to examine domestic issues from the perspectives of others. Green (2002) observed that faculty who have been abroad to study, teach, or lead students have been deeply transformed by the experience. Monk (2000) noted that internationalization means more than increased knowledge, empathy for, and understanding of other social groups. It also requires an emotional, perceptual, and cognitive shift in the personal response to "otherness." The best way to achieve this is through continuous, firsthand, direct immersion. Unfortunately, budget cutbacks and the suspension of international travel on many campuses may make this investment vulnerable.

RESEARCH

The work of international research needs to focus on giving voice to people who have been traditionally left out of paradigm construction.

Research should serve as the vehicle to correct faulty assumptions and stereotypes. This requires critical understanding on the part of researchers of the cultural orientation of research participants. People from different parts of the world may have different conceptualizations of relationships. Our responsibility, as educators in family science, is to develop the skills and sensibilities needed to cross multiple borders. In doing so, we can conduct research that expands our base of knowledge while increasing the potential for liberating those whom we study. Paradigms such as feminist and critical multicultural approaches are needed to direct research that will foster a heightened consciousness among all family science students. This will facilitate the requisite global awareness for work and citizenship in a globally interdependent world.

Epistemology

In the discussion of internationalizing family science programs, it would be hypocritical if our base of knowledge remained Euro-American, derived mostly from Western traditions, ideas, and theoretical constructs. Inherently, this partial knowledge is usually coated with scientific notions that create the appearance of "objective knowledge." However, there are some obvious limitations associated with this approach. First, by adopting this common narrative to explain family life of all people, the field of family science has a limited comparative dimension and has neglected the complexities of human experience. In addition, this purported objective knowledge has been embraced at the expense of the voices echoing from outside the mainstream. Second, family science has emphasized middle-class values, often viewing the structure and dynamics of families from lower socioeconomic status (SES) as pathological and deviant. This Eurocentric perspective diminishes the significance of the social, historical, and cultural contexts in which much of family life is embedded. The role of colonization, racism, and global oppression are often not included in our discussion of family experiences, nor are these concepts used to guide our research. As Smith (1999) pointed out, research itself is a political exercise. She argued that research is oneway in which imperialism and colonization have been, and continue to be, achieved by defining "legitimate knowledge" (p. 5). Third, in the past few decades, there have been discussions on how to transform a family science curriculum to reflect diverse cultures. However, in our estimation, multicultural research has not been adequately incorporated into the mainstream curricula. In fact, these research activities have occurred as isolated efforts that remain on the periphery of mainstream thinking. These limitations, point to the need, in the field of family science, to reconsider the way we construct knowledge and conduct research.

In the past few decades, feminist and critical multicultural researchers have made concerted efforts to include knowledge constructed by people from outside of the mainstream into the discipline. More grassroots work is needed to uncover the voices of others and to bring them into our consciousness. As a discipline, we should encourage, honor, and respect multiple ways of constructing and reporting knowledge.

Methodology

Research methodology is closely related to epistemology. Conventional research methods have usually been based on traditional theoretical frameworks. Theory sets the parameters for the kind of research questions asked and the kind of data obtained. Theory serves as a guide but is, too often, used to protect us from the complexities of reality. In a discipline such as family science, it is vital that we stay true to the complex lived realities of people across different borders. Paradigms and methods that allow the inclusion of richer and more authentic data, grounded in the experiences of families, seem more promising than traditional methodology.

In an attempt to construct a model for the development of culturally competent researchers, Papadopoulos and Lees (2002) advocated that cultural awareness, knowledge, and sensitivity are all essential elements in the training of researchers. In recent times, qualitative research methodology, such as ethnography and participatory research has gained acceptance in family science scholarly inquiry. These approaches are more appropriate tools to characterize selected aspects of family life, but admittedly, are not without problems. In any case, it is necessary for researchers to examine and confront their theoretical and personal values and to recognize that these values are socially constructed.

Furthermore, researchers need to be explicit about their positions in the research process and cognizant of how their cultural background interacts with those they want to study. The formation of a true partnership between researchers and participants is essential for the development of trust. According to Papadopoulos and Lees (2002), true partnerships demand that power relationships and hierarchical relationships are challenged. Thus, this partnering relationship should be reflected in both data collection and data analysis processes.

Gibb (2001) advocated for the importance of collaborative research approaches in social science that are congruent with the worldview of the participants. Such a framework allows researchers to ask questions that are meaningful and informative from the perspectives of the people they are attempting to study. In other words, researchers have to be culturally aware, sensitive, and competent to go beyond traditional theoretical frameworks. Reporting and disseminating findings should be done in such a way as to reach all stakeholder groups and benefit all parties (Papadopoulos & Lees, 2002). In addition, it should be used to inform and broaden our knowledge base. Finally, as classroom instructors, it is vital that we incorporate these research findings into our curricula.

TEACHING PRACTICES AND CURRICULUM

Internationalizing family science education includes operationalizing program goals via learning objectives and specific course content (Green, 2002). It also requires creating learning contexts and teaching strategies that support diversity.

Learning Objectives

Students, including family science undergraduate majors, often enter graduate programs lacking international awareness and competence (Green, 2002; Paige & Williams, 2001) highlighting the need to include international concerns in graduate education. Laesk (1999), as cited in Haigh (2002) targeted six professional competencies for graduates of internationalized programs that can serve as guideposts in program planning. These competencies included:

1. The ability to consider multiple perspectives and worldviews
2. Understanding the mutual influence of local and international dynamics
3. Awareness of one's own worldview
4. Understanding one's profession locally and internationally
5. Valuing multicultural diversity
6. Recognizing the complexities of culture and the intercultural issues relevant to one's profession

The examples we offer in this section highlight how these competencies can inform curricula and teaching practices. We believe that course objectives and classroom activities that help students build these competencies should be integrated throughout the curriculum rather than relegated to a single course. This reflects the belief that culture is important and integral to all areas of education rather than a "special issue." This approach also recognizes that international/multicultural awareness, knowledge, and skill are part of a process that occurs over time and builds on past learning and experiences.

Course Content

It can be very challenging to design courses in ways that serve international concerns, do not rely too heavily on local knowledge, and create positive and relevant learning experiences for all students (Haigh, 2002). Internationalizing must be a multidirectional process that is mutually advantageous, rather than only serving local needs and privileging local worldviews (Yang, 2002). The curriculum needs to include the voices, ideas, and concerns of members of many cultures and nations. It may be difficult to find adequate materials to do this (Garii, 2000) and to decide which readings, assignments, and class exercises to privilege. One resource that is useful in teaching family and child studies from a cross-cultural perspective is Ponzetti's (2003) *International Encyclopedia of Marriage and Family.* Ponzetti's work offers examples of family life in different countries and integrates international scholarship in each entry. Other suggestions for overcoming curriculum limitations include: offering students information on professional organizations in other countries; assigning readings from international journals; and bringing in speakers or panels from various countries to talk about experiences growing up, family traditions, and cultural life ways.

Space also needs to be made in the classroom and in assignments for exploring how the curriculum applies, or fails to apply, to the experience of all students and for meaningful critique of Euro-centered theories. As Green (2002) posited,

> U.S. scientific, economic, and military might; the rise of English as a global language; and the success of our higher education system—as well as its attractiveness to international students—have fueled the American tendency to believe that our own history, language, and culture are all that matter. (p. 12)

Solorzano and Yosso (2001) argued that educational theory and practice informed by dominant U.S. cultural knowledge subordinates members of non-European American groups. Family science curriculum is no exception, as it typically reflects European-American beliefs, values, and norms. This often leaves international students, as well as many U.S. students of color, struggling to find relevancy in what is being presented and/or feeling marginalized or pathologized by the Eurocentric family norms that are the foundation for many theories of family functioning (McDowell, 2003). Educators must consider how curricular choices implicitly or explicitly contribute to or challenge structured power relations (Tisdell, 2001) based in part on the identity of those given voice through readings and class discussions. It can be helpful to have open discussions in the classroom about how some ideas are privileged in family science programs and how this privilege may serve to silence competing ideas and values (McDowell & Shelton, 2002). One technique we have found useful is to post blank paper around the room and ask students to move around and write down those ideas and values they feel are preferred within the program, as well as ideas and values they would feel uncomfortable talking openly about. The class can then discuss as a group.

Learning Context

In order to foster multicultural/international understanding, educators must create diverse learning communities in which multiple perspectives and the lived experience of all students can be explored. To do this, we must create safe learning environments where self-disclosure, self-reflection, honest dialogue, and constructive challenge can occur. Educators need to take nonthreatening postures (Ridley &

Thompson, 1999); set ground rules that ensure students interact with one another in respectful, nonattacking ways (Ramsey, 1999); integrate affective and experiential knowledge with theoretical concepts (Tisdell, 2001); and engage students in activities that promote connection and nurturing while raising consciousness and challenging racist, sexist, heterosexist, and/or nationalist ideologies (Ramsey, 1999). For example, Halevy (1998) introduced an approach to completing a family genogram that helps students identify the origins of their attitudes and collaboratively confront biases. Attitudes about nationality can be included in this exercise. Challenging learners to carefully examine their own ethnocentrism and prejudices may uncover anxiety, vulnerability, ignorance, misinformation, and even hostility (Ridley & Thompson, 1999). This requires careful and sensitive responses from educators (Cheatham, 1999; Kiselica, 1999). To create this kind of learning environment, educators need to lead the way by becoming internationally informed and consciously consider their own cultural identity development and *emic* perspective (i.e., cultural-specific assumptions, values, beliefs, and biases) (Mobley, 1999). It is important to note that how we think about internation- alization itself depends on our own cultural context (Yang, 2002) and deserves our attention as educators.

Teaching Strategies

Specific teaching strategies depend on the competencies being targeted. For example, to help students increase their awareness of their own worldviews and value multicultural diversity educators must find the proper mix of didactic and experiential learning techniques (Cheatham, 1999; Kiselica, 1999). This allows students to tap into their lived experience and increase their self-awareness (Ramsey, 1999) to confront their own biases (D'Andrea & Daniels, 1999). Learning strategies might include activities such as small-group interaction, learning journals, role-plays, Web board discussions, cultural genograms, dyadic interviews, film reviews (McDowell & Shelton, 2002), analysis of the media, guest speakers (Crowley-Long, 1995), personal narratives (Curtis, 1998), immersion experiences (Pope-Davis, Breaus, & Liu, 1998), and community service work (D'Andrea & Daniels, 1999).

A more in-depth example is an assignment we have given that helps students discover the international influences in their own lives. We asked students to apply family studies literature to describe and compare their own development with that of someone from a different nation/culture. Multiple international competencies are targeted in this assignment, including encouraging students to consider multiple perspectives/worldviews; realize the influence of local and international dynamics; become more aware of their own worldviews; value multicultural diversity; and recognize the complexities of how culture is relevant to their work with families. This assignment can be completed in a number of ways to enhance these learning competencies. For example, students from different backgrounds can work in dyads comparing their experiences and researching/critiquing the literature regarding development in each of their perspective cultures. Students can consider the historic international influences on their development. For instance, African-American students might explore the contemporary effects of slavery; indigenous students might consider the effects of European imperialism/colonization; and European-American students might consider the impact of immigration and their mixed national heritage.

The following excerpts are from a paper Christina Holland wrote while enrolled in the course. She chose to compare and contrast the influences of her own lived international experience.

CASE EXAMPLE:
DISCOVERING INTERNATIONAL INFLUENCES

I am as much Vietnamese as I am "American" (Irish/English) but throughout my life I have faced invisible obstacles rooted in the conflict between my two cultures. My mother met and married my American father while living in Saigon. The thought of an interracial marriage was unacceptable to my [maternal] grandmother as well as the culture at large. Many people had feelings of anger toward the relationships between American men and Vietnamese women during the war (Cullinan, 2001). I was born in Thailand and we moved to the United States when I was three only to face my father's unemployment, alcoholism, and violent abuse. My mother was left with no choice but to ask for help from my Vietnamese family who had recently settled in San Francisco. The reunion was humiliating and she had to literally beg to be allowed back into the family. I embodied everything my grandmother feared for her daughter, and now we were at her mercy . . . Vietnamese family relationships are far different from the Western ideals of family. Vietnamese culture is both hierarchical and male dominated with a strong emphasis on family, which may consist of multiple, extended, and cross-generational members. Sometimes two or three generations reside in one household (Galanti, 2000). This was the case when I was growing up. Vietnamese families have a tendency for siblings to pool resources in providing care for family members (McLaggen, 2002). My mother and aunt combined their paychecks to help support all the members in the household where priority was placed on family interests over individual desires (Pyke, 2000). From a Western point of view we were probably considered a poor immigrant family, but from the Vietnamese cultural lens, we were merely carrying over a native tradition, with one major difference. We weren't in Vietnam anymore . . . my racially mixed appearance was seen with two overlapping and confusing lenses. On the one hand I was My Lai or mixed (reference to the My Lai massacre in Vietnam where U.S. troops murdered an entire village of innocents), which represented all the worst images of the Vietnam War. But on the other hand I was pretty and spoke English well, which was a source of pride for my family. I was biracial, an outsider . . . Vietnamese children face a daunting school experience where language difficulties, racial inequality, and exposure to an often adversarial youth subculture pose serious physical and developmental threats (Barlow, 2001). These same obstacles remained present during my transition from childhood into early adulthood. The struggle to shape an identity both physically and mentally was encumbered by mixed messages of who I was supposed to be inside versus outside of the family. My complex intercultural/international history has shaped my perspective by fashioning several lenses for me to look through. My ability to recognize multiple facets of the same issue can only help my future work with families.

This assignment exemplifies ways to highlight the relevance of international relationships in all of our lives. Furthermore, it brings learners together in a commonly defined global community.

STUDENT BODY

Instructors should emphasize that all students and faculty are "international" with respect to global influences in our lives. None of us is without an international group history. For example, everyone in the United States originally emigrated from another country, was brought from their home country by force, or was indigenous and deeply impacted by the arrival of members of other nations. At the same time, we believe it is beneficial to all program participants to have a diverse student body that includes students from outside the United States. This allows multidirectional learning, opportunities to critique Euro-centered theories, and cross-cultural understanding.

Recruitment

The admission processes of some family science programs may have significant barriers for international students. For example, it is not uncommon for graduate programs to require an in-person interview or to offer assistantships after students have committed to attending. It is necessary for students from some countries to secure work in the United States before a student visa is granted. Offering assistantships as part of an acceptance package can determine the ability of these students to accept an offer. Interviewing in person can be cost prohibitive. We have found it helpful to interview using Instant Messaging and/or to send prospective students a series of questions and ask that they videotape their answers. Videotape can be particularly useful, as it allows faculty one way to assess the language skills of ESL (English as a second language) applicants. Frequent e-mail communication with prospective international students is also useful, not only to help answer their many questions, but to begin to develop a personal connection they can rely on when making their transition to a new culture (McDowell et al., 2002).

Support

Family science programs that recruit and admit international students have an obligation to carefully consider how ready they are to offer these students a relevant and successful learning experience (Haigh, 2002). They must make concerted efforts to support international students who may be at a disadvantage in relationship to language and culture. English-speaking students and international students who come from countries where English is mainstream have an advantage. Differences in preferred speech patterns (e.g., slow and thoughtful versus fast-paced) can also pose obstacles to international students. Likewise, U.S. students and students from Westernized countries are privileged via their understanding of the local context. This is particularly true in fields such as family science that are highly language and culture dependent.

International students entering family science graduate programs may feel on the margins of the student body. They have reported feeling at a loss when colleagues and educators make reference to historical events and cultural experiences unique to the United States. Some have reported feeling that their graduate program "belonged" to native students. International students have also reported feeling "othered" by faculty and peers who conspicuously failed to acknowledge cultural differences, and/or engaged in shallow conversations about such things as how long they had been in the Unites States, their home-country cuisine, or how well they spoke English. Likewise, international students, who often have class privilege in their home countries, have reported being discriminated against for the first time when they entered the United States to study. Though more overt discrimination tends to occur outside of their educational programs, international students have also reported being marginalized by faculty who may underestimate their abilities or see them as having come from "lesser" countries. Finally, international students have reported struggling to apply Eurocentric theories and practices to families in their home countries (McDowell et al., 2003; McDowell, 2003).

Faculty members need to find ways to promote connection and inclusion of international students. Faculty and/or current students meeting with incoming international students may help in encouraging a smooth transition. Student "buddies" can also be assigned to help international students find housing, get oriented to the community and program, and build personal connections. International students for whom English is a second or third language may also need time to process what is being said in group and classroom contexts to have true opportunities for their voices to be heard. Additional suggestions include: offering international students meaningful assistantships within programs, assigning group projects and encouraging inclusive study groups in courses, making space in classroom discussions for one-on-one and nonpressured group dialogue, spending time talking with students outside of the classroom, and encouraging research and assignments that include application to students' countries of origin.

One of the successful strategies used to support international students has been to invite them to participate in student dialogue groups that targeted cross-racial and cross-cultural understanding (McDowell et al., 2003). Cross-cultural dialogue can promote the kind of boundary crossing that allows for new understanding, meaning, and knowledge to be created (Tastsoglou, 2000) helping to build international competencies such as considering multiple perspectives, understanding international dynamics, increasing cultural self-awareness, valuing diversity, and exploring the professional relevance of culture. Following is a brief description of our experience.

CASE EXAMPLE: DIALOGUE GROUP

Dialogue group members included U.S. white students and students of color as well as international students. Group members agreed on "ground rules" to create and maintain a safe environment in which to build relationships and disclose personal experiences. Members frequently explored the influence of their own intersecting identities of race, nationality, gender, sexual orientation, language, education, class, etc., on their experiences of being privileged and/or marginalized in the United States and their home countries. For international students, coming to the United States was often their first and only experience of being marginalized and seen as "other." The dialogue group became a place where these students could express their confusion and emotional reactions to things that happened in or out of their educational programs, such as having their accents mocked, being asked by others to speak for their entire country, having language deficits misinterpreted as deficits in cognitive ability, hearing negative comments about people from their country, and many other negative comments. International students in these groups were also able to form intimate connections with other participants, increasing their sense of belonging. Finally, the dialogue groups made space for more careful investigation into how what students were learning could or could not be applied in various cultural contexts. These types of efforts, which at times go beyond the classroom, help build plural and inclusive learning communities.

CONCLUSION

Internationalization of family science programs remains a work in progress. In a discipline that has tremendous importance in working with families and children, many profound changes must occur. These changes are essential if we are to be entrusted with making a major shift to a higher level of engagement and commitment to the welfare of families and children in the world. An internationalized family science program means creating better and more equal learning opportunities for all students. We need to do more than simply recruit more international students to join family science programs. We must create and maintain pluralistic learning environments at all levels of the institution. As suggested by Haigh (2002), internationalization of any program in higher education goes beyond just teaching and learning. It requires a substantial reevaluation of all institutional activities. A truly successful program requires internationalizing the institution, faculty, student body, research, teaching practices, and curriculum.

REFERENCES

Altbach, P. (2002). Perspectives on international higher education. *Change, 34,* 29-31.
Barlow, D. (2001). Growing up American: How Vietnamese children adapt to the United States. *The Educational Digest, 66,* 76-77.
Cheatham, H. (1999). Where do we go from here? Some observations and recommendations for multicultural educators. In M. Kiselica (Ed.), *Confronting prejudice and racism during multicultural training* (pp. 171-179). Alexandra, VA: American Counseling Association.
Crowley-Long, K. (1995). Resources for teaching white students about issues of race. *Clearing House, 68,* 134-138.
Cullinan, C. (2001). Becoming American. *The World & I, 16,* 178-185.
Curtis, C. (1998). Creating culturally responsive curriculum: Making race matter. *Clearing House, 7,* 135-139.
D'Andrea, M. & Daniels, J. (1999). Exploring the psychology of white racism through naturalistic inquiry. *Journal of Counseling and Development, 77,* 93-101.
Dilys, S. (2000). What really do we mean by internationalization? *Contemporary Education, 71,* 5-12.
Galanti, G. (2000). Vietnamese family relationships. *Western Journal of Medicine, 172,* 415-417.
Garii, B. (2000). U.S. social studies in the 21st century: Internationalizing the curriculum for global citizens. *Social Studies, 91,* 257-264.
Gibb, M. (2001). Toward a strategy for undertaking cross-cultural collaborative research. *Society and Natural Resources, 14,* 673-687.
Gloria, A. & Pope-Davis, D. (1998). Cultural ambivalence: The importance of a culturally aware learning environment in the training and education of counselors. In D. Pope-Davis & H. Coleman (Eds.), *Multicultural counseling competencies: Assessment, education and training, and supervision* (pp. 242-262). Thousand Oaks, CA: Sage.
Green, M. F. (2002). Joining the world: The challenge of internationalizing undergraduate education. *Change, 34,* 12-21.
Haigh, M. (2002). Internationalization of the curriculum: Designing inclusive education for a small world. *Journal of Geography in Higher Education, 26,* 49-66.
Halevy, J. (1998). A genogram with an attitude. *Journal of Marital and Family Therapy, 24* (2), 233-242.

Hayward, F. M. (1995). International opportunities and challenges for American higher education in Africa, Asia, and Latin America. In K. H. Hanson & J.W. Meryerson (Eds.), *International challenges to American colleges and universities: Looking ahead* (pp. 117-140). Phoenix: Oryx.

Kiselica, M. (1999). Reducing prejudice: The role of the empathetic-confrontive instructor. In M. Kiselica (Ed.), *Confronting prejudice and racism during multicultural training* (pp. 137-154). Alexandra, VA: American Counseling Association.

McDowell, T. (2003). Professional education and critical race theory: Exploring the experiences of graduate trainees. Unpublished doctoral dissertation. Northern Illinois University, DeKalb, IL.

McDowell, T., Fang, S., Brownlee, K., Gomez Young, C., & Khanna, A. (2002). Transforming a MFT program: A model for enhancing diversity. *Journal of Marital and Family Therapy, 28,* 179-191.

McDowell, T., Fang, S., Gomez Young, C., Khanna, A., Sherman, B., & Brownlee, K. (2003). Making space for racial dialogue: Our experience in a MFT training program. *Journal of Marital and Family Therapy, 29,* 179-194.

McDowell, T. & Shelton, D. (2002). Valuing ideas of social justice in MFT curricula. *Journal of Contemporary Family Therapy, 24,* 313-331.

McLaggan, C. (2002). We live both lives. Special to *The American Statesman,* September 29, 2002.

McNairy, F. G. (1996). The challenge for higher education: Retaining students of color. *New Directions for Student Services, 47,* 3-14.

Mobley, M., in collaboration with H. Cheatham. (1999). R.A.C.E.-Racial affirmation and counselor educators. In M. Kiselica (Ed.), *Confronting prejudice and racism during multicultural training* (pp. 89-106). Alexandra, VA: American Counseling Association.

Monk, J. (2000). Looking out, looking in-in the Journal of Geography in Higher Education. *Journal of Geography in Higher Education, 24,* 163-177.

Paige, R. & Williams, S. (2001). Perceptions of university seniors toward internationalizing curriculum in family and consumer sciences: Have we made progress? *Journal of Family & Consumer Sciences, 93,* 79-83.

Papadopoulos, I. & Lees, S. (2002). Developing culturally competent researchers. *Journal of Advanced Nursing, 37,* 258-266.

Ponzetti, Jr., J. J. (Ed.). (2003) *International encyclopedia of marriage and family* (Second ed., Vols. 1-4). New York: Macmillan Press.

Pope-Davis, D., Breaus, C., & Liu, W. (1998). A multicultural immersion experience: Filling the void in multicultural training. In D. Pope-Davis & H. Coleman (Eds.), *Multicultural counseling competencies: Assessment, education and training, and supervision* (pp. 227-241). Thousand Oaks, CA: Sage.

Pyke, K. (2000). The normal American family as an interpretive structure of family life among grown children of Korean and Vietnamese immigrants. *Journal of Youth and Adolescence, 30,* 135-153.

Ramsey, M. (1999). How to create a climate for cultural diversity appreciation within the classroom. In M. Kiselica (Ed.), *Confronting prejudice and racism during multicultural training* (pp. 112-136). Alexandra, VA: American Counseling Association.

Ridley, C. & Thompson, C. (1999). Managing resistance to diversity training: A social systems perspective. In M. Kiselica (Ed.), *Confronting prejudice and racism during multicultural training* (pp. 74-92). Alexandra, VA: American Counseling Association.

Smith, T. L. (1999). *Decolonizing methodologies: Research and indigenous peoples.* Dunedin, New Zealand: University of Otago.

Solorzano, D. & Yosso, T. (2001). From racial stereotyping and deficit discourse toward a critical race theory in teacher education. *Multicultural Education, 9,* 2-8.

Tastsoglou, E. (2000). Mapping the unknowable: The challenges and rewards of cultural, political and pedagogical border crossing. In G. Dei & A. Calliste (Eds.), *Power, knowledge and anti-racism education* (pp. 98-121). Hallifaz, Nova Scotia: Fernwood Publishing.

Tisdell, E. (2001). The politics of positionality: Teaching for social change in higher education. In R. Cervero & A. Wilson (Eds.), *Power in practice* (pp. 145-163). San Francisco: Josey Bass.

Vazquez, L. (1998). A systemic multicultural curriculum model: The pedagogical process. In D. Pope-Davis & H. Coleman (Eds.), *Multicultural counseling competencies: Assessment, education and training, and supervision* (pp. 159-183). Thousand Oaks, CA: Sage.

Yang, R. (2002). University internationalization: Its meanings, rationales and implications. *Intercultural Education, 13,* 81-95.

Chapter 2

Cultural Lessons in Sexuality:
Comparison of Parent-Child
Communication Styles
in Three Cultures

Carol Anderson Darling
Stacy N. Howard

A cross-cultural perspective is needed when we teach about families. Since many students attending American universities have an ethnocentric view of culture, it is important to provide an alternative perspective that is not focused specifically on one's own culture, but rather one that provides an ethnorelative approach. Whether teaching about family relations, family communication, parent education, or sexuality, cultural differences and implications can enhance learning within our own culture, as well as learning about other cultures. Providing a cross-cultural approach is important because it allows us to go beyond a narrow focus of Western culture and concepts. We need to create a climate within our family sciences classes that fosters thinking not only about family content, but also multicultural understanding.

Although some family science departments have specific courses in cultural diversity, cultural learning can be infused into a variety of courses and topics. To better understand and enhance a multicultural perspective in our family science courses, a circular role-play teaching method addressing parenting and parent-child communication about sexuality has been utilized in three cultural settings. Employing this teaching method and discussing the results from other cultures have been found to stimulate cultural learning and understandings about the purposes underlying behaviors, so we can more readily

doi:10.1300/5609_02

21

apply a broad perspective of families and human interaction. Sexuality, as it is understood in the United States, often bears little resemblance to sexual relationships and practices across cultures (Blackwood, 2000). Therefore, by looking at cultural evidence from three different countries, this teaching and research endeavor facilitated the exploration of the richness and diversity of parent-child communication concerning sexuality issues from a broader perspective. Furthermore, considering the variations from others' experiences should help put our own parenting and sexual understandings in perspective.

Culture is a powerful force in shaping how we feel and behave as parents, children, and sexual beings. Beginning at birth, individuals are socialized into their particular culture and taught the values, beliefs, and behaviors that will permit them to successfully function within it (Gardiner, Mutter, & Kosmitzki, 1998). As part of this socialization process, children from an early age learn to conform to the roles that culture considers consistent with their biological sex, including the rules surrounding communications about gender, and especially sexuality. One's sexual life is connected with the structure of society including its values, norms, and habits of its people. Thus, both sexuality and parenting related to sexual learning can have extraordinarily different meanings to people depending on cultural influences.

Distinct biological and cultural markers indicate a readiness among women and men to find a sexual partner; however, these biological and cultural indicators may or may not coincide, depending on cultural norms. Across cultures, adolescent experiences vary greatly in terms of how strictly adolescents are guided by cultural values and which forms behaviors take (Gardiner, Mutter, & Kosmitzki, 1998). As a result, adolescents in many cultures are permitted to explore and express their sexuality in a variety of ways. Buss (1989) found that cultures disagreed more on the value of premarital sexual experience (or inexperience) than on any other issue. In China, India, Indonesia, Iran, Israel (the Palestinian Arabs), and Taiwan, young people were insistent that chastity was "indispensable" in a partner. In contrast, men and women from Finland, France, Norway, the Netherlands, Sweden, and West Germany were equally likely to insist that chastity was relatively unimportant. Other researchers have found similar results. For example, generally, young people in Asia, Mexico, the Middle East, and South America strongly disapprove of premarital sexual activity. On the other hand, young adults in the United States,

Belgium, France, and the Scandinavian countries hold relatively permissive sexual standards (Alzate, 1984; Christensen, 1973; Iwawaki & Eysenck, 1978; Kontula & Haavio-Mannila, 1995; LaBeff & Dodder, 1982; Shapurian & Hojat, 1985; Werebe & Reinert, 1983).

After decades of research, adolescent sexuality has been linked to personality, and biological, demographic, social, and cultural influences. Furthermore, experts emphasize the key role of parents as primary agents of sexual socialization. Considerable research on how parents affect adolescent sexual behavior has been directed toward communication, that is, examining parents' explicit attempts to transmit values and share information (Miller, Benson, & Galbraith, 2001). Recent investigations have demonstrated that parents' sexual values, in combination with parent-child communication, have an important effect on adolescents' intercourse experiences (Jaccard, Dittus, & Gordon, 1996; Luster & Small, 1997; Miller, Norton, Fan, & Christopherson, 1998; Miller et al., 1999). According to Raffaelli and Green (2003), this body of research reinforces the role of parent-child communication in shaping adolescent sexual attitudes and behaviors. However, at the same time, the researchers suggested that much remains to be learned about how parents communicate with their children about sexual issues, particularly in ethnically diverse families.

Cultural context is important in understanding parenting, parent-child communication, and sexuality. To better understand the cultural influences in the three cultures pertinent to this study, some background information about Costa Rica, Finland, and the United States has been included.

Within a research context, the purpose of this investigation was to determine if parents in Costa Rica, Finland, and the United States have different styles of parenting and communicate differently to their children about sexuality. Specific research questions include what types of communication styles exist between parents and children in these three cultures and what is the content of these communications.

COSTA RICA

Although Costa Rica has a higher standard of living than many Latin American nations and occupies a middle position in terms of per-capita income, it shows more development in social indices.

Costa Rica has one of the highest literacy rates in Latin America, one of the lowest children's mortality rates per 100,000 people, and one of the highest life expectancy rates (Schifter & Madrigal, 2000). Notwithstanding the good achievements in health and social security, approximately one-third of the population lives below the poverty line (as cited by Schifter & Madrigal, 2000). The country of Costa Rica shares with the rest of the region problems of unemployment, urban decay, increasing crime rates, and drug-related problems.

Sexual practices in Costa Rica are not much different from those of the rest of Latin America. For a snapshot, consider the following data: 42 percent of births take place outside of marriage; 18 percent of unwed mothers are nineteen years of age or younger; almost half of all pregnancies are unwanted, on average; and 20 percent of marriages end in divorce (as cited by Schifter & Madrigal, 2000).

In regard to young people's sources of information about sexuality, researchers of the First National Survey on AIDS, as documented by Schifter and Madrigal (2000), indicated that for almost half of young male respondents (fifteen-twenty-four years), the street was where most of their sexuality education occurred. The situation is somewhat different for young women, with home (34 percent) and school (26 percent) being the principal sources of information. Other sources for both male and female respondents were books, magazines, and newspapers. As for the question of whom young people talk to about sex, young men tended to confide mainly in their friends and classmates (64 percent), while only 7 percent discussed sexual issues with their parents. In contrast, young women were more communicative, confiding in their mothers (29 percent), husbands (27 percent), and friends and classmates (23 percent). With regard to the level of intimacy in these discussions, it was found to be generally low between fathers and their children (less than 35 percent for males and less than 20 percent for females), and highest between mothers and daughters, and between male respondents and their male friends or classmates (Schifter & Madragil, 2000).

FINLAND

Various social changes have occurred within the Finnish culture during the past fifty years, such as a rise in the level of education and an increase in urbanization. Along with these changes there has been an increase in the income level and the standard of living of families. However, an important enduring element in Finnish society is the equal and more independent position of women compared to other countries in the world. Thus, examining sexuality in a more egalitarian society, such as Finland, can lead to further understanding for other cultures as they progress toward equality for men and women (Darling, Haavio-Mannila, & Kontula, 2001).

Although Finland has a high degree of equality between men and women, equality is a complicated issue and several generations will undoubtedly pass before it is achieved. Within the Finnish culture, there is a real commitment to valuing families and parenthood. Family size is carefully planned, with the number of children per family averaging 1.7 across the Finnish population (Taipale, 1995). Sixty percent of the births are family deliveries, during which fathers are present, and about 46 percent of fathers use their right to take two weeks of paternity leave after a baby is born. Finnish girls are encouraged to be bold, sensitive, or shy and are cherished by parents just as much as Finnish boys. Girls can grow up to be independent, have control over their own lives, and live in an environment in which sex is something that can be discussed. As a result, teenage pregnancy is not as big a problem as it is in many Western countries. In fact, the average age when young men and women experience their first intercourse is approximately eighteen years of age, which is somewhat later than that of U.S. teens (Kontula & Haavio-Mannila, 1995).

Research into Finnish sexuality shows that the generation of Finns who experienced the sexual revolution was born between 1937-1956 and experienced their youth between 1950 and 1970, when the gender gap still favored men (Ojanlatva, Helenius, Rautava, Ahvenainen, & Koskenvuo, 2003). Although limited, sexual information was available in science magazines and books, however, only men told sexual stories. It was not until the generation of gender equalization (born between 1957-1973) that the ideas of the sexual revolution were realized. Information and experience became acceptable for both genders, but information was still not readily available to women and talking about sexuality was still not as acceptable for women as it was for men.

Today, women still continue to perceive the combination of love and sex as the best alternative, although some men are also beginning to agree. According to Kontula and Haavio-Mannila (1995) the more satisfied Finnish individuals were with their sexual lives, the easier it was to communicate about sexuality. Furthermore, researchers suggested that the attitudes of men and women have become significantly closer, attitudes toward premarital sex have become more liberal, and the right of women to take sexual initiative is more commonly met with approval.

First sexual intercourse was perceived as a symbol of growing up for many Finnish youth. Kontula and Haavio-Mannila (1995) found that a significant change occurred during the past decades regarding the age of first intercourse. From the 1930s to the beginning of the 1980s, ever younger individuals were having intercourse for the first time, with the age of first intercourse in 1992 being 17.9 for females and 18.1 for males. Kontula and Haavio-Mannila suggest that the diminishing gender gap not only occurs in various sectors of life such as education, work, family, and leisure time, but also sexuality.

UNITED STATES

Adolescent sexuality in the United States has changed considerably over the past fifty years (Joyner & Laumann, 2001). After World War II, adolescents were more focused on going to school, entering the work force, getting married, and beginning a family. However, with such social changes as the introduction of oral contraceptives, legalized abortions, feminism, and postponement of marriage, refusing to engage in sexual intercourse prior to marriage lost some of its appeal. These cultural changes also influenced the reduction of adolescent inhibitions regarding sexuality. Moreover, noncoital sex is also common among teens because it is perceived as a way to have sex without the loss of virginity or risk of pregnancy, along with a lower possibility of transmitting STDs (Remez, 2000).

The U.S. population is comprised of many ethnic and cultural groups with varying economic and social conditions. For example, Asian Americans are less likely to engage in premarital sex than are Latin Americans, African Americans, or whites (Cochran, Mays, & Leung, 1991). Furthermore, Latin-American culture often endorses sexual exploration for males while placing a high value on chastity before marriage for women (Comas-Diaz, 1987). However, such differences are generalities, not universal truths about groups of people, diversity can exist within subgroups. Sexual topics are often taboo.

Children and adolescents are discouraged from obtaining sexual knowledge, but, also, a double standard exists between females and males.

Whether or not adolescents become involved in any sexual interactions, they are still sexual people and sexuality is central to their identity development. Therefore, adolescence becomes a time of both confusion and sexual exploration. For adolescents, issues surrounding puberty require an endless amount of attention, because many teens experience the onset of anxiety, turmoil, excitement, and an unavoidable dread (McCann & Petrich-Kelly, 1999). During middle and late adolescence, a greater number of youths engage in heterosexual intercourse. According to the Centers for Disease Control and Prevention (2000), in 1999 approximately half of the students in grades nine to twelve reported having experienced intercourse (48 percent females and 52 percent males). Compared to women thirty years ago, females are engaging in first intercourse at younger ages (Trussell & Vaughn, 1991). As a result, adolescents experience some conflict between identity, especially gender identity, and role confusion; at the same time they are also trying to learn how to manage physical and emotional intimacy.

Today, teens can be bombarded by the media (television, movies, music, and the Internet), which provide increasingly frequent portrayals of sexuality (Brown, 2002). Although there is increasing public concern about the potential of health risks of early, unprotected sexual activity, most of the mass media rarely depict the "three Cs" of responsible sexual behavior: commitment, contraceptives, and consideration of consequences (Kunkel, et al., 1999). Thus, the influence of media becomes a challenge for parents and educators.

Several family variables influence adolescent sexual and contraceptive behavior (Miller, 2002). When adults and teens openly talk about sexuality, teens are more likely to delay first intercourse and if they are sexually active, they are more likely to use contraceptives or have fewer partners (Hogan & Kitagawa, 1985; Jaccard, Dittus, & Gordon, 1996; Miller, 1998; Resnick et al., 1997; Upchurch, Aneshensel, Sucoff, & Levy-Storms, 1999). In comparison, parental control can be associated with negative effects if it is excessive or coercive (Miller, 1998). Although young adults reported wishing their parents had shared more information with them about sexuality, parents are often unsure and uncomfortable with this role (Hutchinson & Cooney, 1998). Thus, parents need to personalize their sexual communications to each child's needs. Regardless if we agree with actions, beliefs, or attitudes of today's youths, it cannot be ignored that countless teens are engaging in a variety of sexual behaviors with a range of results and consequences. Youths need to be provided with accurate information, values clarification, and parental guidance in order to help them in their decision-making responsibilities concerning their sexuality (Darling & Hollon, 2002).

TEACHING METHODOLOGY

The learning experience consisted of a circular role-play in which a paragraph was read to the class and each student was asked to consecutively respond as both a parent and an adolescent in simultaneous role-play responses. Students were asked to form a small circle of six to eight persons and bring with them a sheet of paper and pencil. The following was read to them.

> As parents you are going away to the mountains for a weekend alone. Your daughter, Kim, who is fourteen years old and nearly fifteen, is going to stay at home. She prepares supper, does her chores, and sits down to watch television. She decides to call her boyfriend to join her in watching television. After you drive for two hours you get to the base of the mountain, but have car trouble. You are told that your car will not make it up the mountain, so you decide to return home. When you arrive home, one parent is putting the car in the garage while the other goes in to find the daughter and her boyfriend, Steve, on the couch in a nude embrace.

After the scenario was presented, students were asked to respond by portraying the roles of the parents and then the daughter. It is important to note that the participants in this learning experience were students and not necessarily parents or daughters in real life, however, they were asked to play the roles of the parent and daughter. To facilitate the explanation of this activity within this exercise, the abbreviated terminology of parent and daughter may at times be used to signify the parent and daughter roles that the students were portraying.

The participants in the small groups were first asked to take the role of the parent who found the daughter in the nude embrace and write on paper what he or she would say to the daughter. After completing this statement, the parent was asked to pass the comment to the person playing the role of the daughter, who was to his or her right. The participants, who were now in the daughter role, were asked to write a reaction to the initial parental statement. When this statement was completed, the student, who was role-playing the daughter, was asked to give a response to the person on his or her left, or the parent figure who wrote the original statement. The parent was asked to write a follow-up statement to the daughter and pass it to the daughter on the right. The daughter was then asked to respond to the parent one more time and give the statement back to the parent. Thus, each individual was playing the role of a parent and daughter simultaneously in two different hypothetical family scenarios. The parent and daughter characters each wrote comments twice, due to time limitations, although this exchange could have occurred several more times.

Following this exercise, the instructor facilitated a discussion and incorporated various questions as prompts to enhance the discussion. Only those questions that were pertinent to the flow of the discussion were incorporated. Following are some examples of questions that could be integrated regarding issues related to first reactions, youth expectations, gender, age, and styles of communication and parenting.

First Reactions

- What was your "first" reaction to the situation? How important are first reactions?
- In your parental role, did you react from your head or on impulse? Was the first reaction of the person in the parental role calm and rational or upset and out of control?
- Did either the parent or daughter characters invoke the deity, such as "Oh my God!" or use strong words that would result in escalating symmetry between the adolescent and parent?
- Did the parent figure instruct the daughter and boyfriend to get dressed or was the parent in such an outrage that this idea did not present itself?
- When playing the parental role did you display emotional and intellectual control or did you revert to scripts from your own parents?

Youths' Expectations

- Should adolescents have the freedom to express their sexuality?
- Should adolescents have the right to privacy?

Gender

- Would the person in the parental role react similarly or differently if one were to find a son in a nude embrace?
- How might the gender of the person playing the parental and adolescent daughter roles have influenced his or her responses?

Age

- Would the age of the adolescent affect how parents handle situations dealing with emerging sexuality at ages 14, 15, 16, 17, 18, or young adults living in the home? If so, how?
- How would the age of the person playing the parental and daughter roles influence his or her reactions to this scenario?

Styles of Communication and Parenting

- What values were expressed in the interactions between the characters portraying the parent and daughter?
- Were parents communicating values, rules, or both, and how did these values influence the messages that were communicated?
- Did the interactions involve power and control, blaming, intellectualizing, contrition, embarrassment, trust or breach of trust, and/or calmness and civility?
- Were the persons role-playing the parent able to respond immediately or did they need some time and space to become calm and contemplate what to do?
- How did the parental characters deal with the boyfriend and his parents?
- What is the role of parents in teaching about responsibility, accountability, and meaningful relationships?
- Did the parental characters make themselves vulnerable, use communication enhancers, or try alternate strategies of parenting than typically used?

- How do parents give positive sex messages to their teens, male and female, and at what age do parents give specific sexuality messages?

After the discussion regarding parenting, parent-child communications, and communicating with adolescents about sexuality in the culture in which the course was taught, the general themes portrayed in other cultures were integrated into the conversation. These cultural additions to the discussion were expanded as this learning experience was used in other cultures and new data and insights were gleaned. Students in all three cultures responded with surprise and amazement regarding alternative ways that other cultures had approached these issues. Although the responses to the discussion were not recorded, the reactions were similar for males and females and across cultures. As a result, the discussion turned from an ethnocentric perspective to an ethnorelative approach.

RESEARCH METHODOLOGY

Sample

The sample consisted of students in a social science course dealing with families and interpersonal relations in Costa Rica, Finland, and the United States. There were fifteen students from Costa Rica, twenty-three students from Finland, and twenty-three students from the United States. There were sixty students in the U.S. class, but a random sample was drawn of the U.S. students to equal the size of the Finnish class. Though the classes in all three countries had both males and females, there were more females in each class. Since there were no names on the papers or gender identification, specific demographics were not available. Generally, the students ranged in age from twenty to thirty.

Data Collection

In an attempt to more broadly explore the communication constructs found in the students' role-playing activity, a qualitative research method was selected. By utilizing qualitative research methodologies, this study was better equipped to investigate a little-understood phenomenon by searching for major themes that emerged from the transcribed role-play sessions (Bogdan & Biklen, 1992; Cresswell, 1998, 2003; Strauss & Corbin, 1990).

These data evolved from a learning experience presented in three cultures, which allowed comparison of cross-cultural approaches to parenting and especially communication related to sexuality. Though the essential content of the situation remained the same in each country including the researcher/educator, the names of the hypothetical parent and daughter in the role-play scenario were changed to reflect common names in that culture (Costa Rica, "Elena" and "Carlos"; Finland, "Sari" and "Antti"; United States, "Kim and Steve"). The data were derived only from the written comments of the participants, who were later asked to submit their written interactive comments to the instructor/researcher following this activity. The anonymous responses were typed and compared with handwritten responses to ensure accuracy. Constant comparative analyses were implemented through the entire frame of the study (Janesick, 1994). The data were analyzed by one primary researcher using data sets from all three countries during the same time frame. The process involved continually categorizing, sorting, and coding data to identify relevant information and major themes (Denzin & Lincoln, 1994, 1998b; Miles & Huberman, 1994). Furthermore, content analysis was also utilized, which refers to any qualitative data reduction and sense-making effort that takes a volume of qualitative material and attempts to identify core consistencies and meanings (Patton, 2002). These core consistencies are generally referred to as patterns or themes.

Particular attention was paid to those experiences that underlie growth and development of understanding—how individuals develop meanings and perspectives (Denzin & Lincoln, 1998a). Investigator triangulation was utilized to verify the themes by incorporating and comparing the independent analyses of the same data (Cresswell, 1998; Janesick, 1994). The intent of using the data from these assignments was not to provide statistically generalizable quantitative results, but to provide a cultural context and meaning to facilitate an understanding of our own cultural experiences, illuminate new interpretations and possible patterns of relationships, and provide insightful examples.

RESULTS

A variety of major themes were drawn from the students' responses and reactions during the role-play conversations. The styles and messages in each of the role-play conversations were important in understanding how the students participating in the activity developed meaning around the given circumstances. Major themes were identified within each cultural set of role-play data and both similarities and differences were uncovered within the examined cultural groups. The larger categorization of themes was structured around two broader categories: parenting and sexuality. Subthemes, such as trust, love, contraception, and peer pressure, were placed in the larger categories in order to draw expanded meaning from the activity and to provide more targeted implications for classroom discussion. Independent quotes from respondents have been included to exemplify themes; however, the quotes are not part of an ongoing dialogue, rather each statement represents one response in any given role-play activity.

Parenting

Analysis of the role-play conversations offered insight into the different approaches students portraying parents utilized in communicating with their role-play daughters about sensitive and difficult topics. Although parents varied in their approaches, various themes emerged from each culture including their first reactions, which ranged from apologetic to furious. Finnish parents played more apologetic roles and approached the situations they interrupted with more caution. Their conversations were also more accepting of the daughter's behaviors as compared to the more upset or shocked Costa Rican and American parents. Finnish parents expressed their concerns in apologetic ways by saying, "Sorry to interrupt you, the car broke down" or "I think this would not have happened because I would have made heaps of noise when entering the house." In contrast, American parents' first reactions were either, e.g., "Oh, my God!" or "What in God's name are you doing?" These derogatory terms were quite varied and were used several times. An angry tone was notably present in the American student responses.

Costa Rican parents more often communicated the concepts of trust and consequences concerning their daughters' behaviors compared to the other two cultural groups. Moreover, the Costa Rican parental responses were the only statements that specifically identified consequences, such as the daughter's educational plans and future career goals. This trend suggests that in the given sample, the Costa Rican respondents in the parental roles utilized an approach that focused on a long-term perspective, as compared to respondents from the Finnish and American parental roles, who maintained a present-focused approach. In the scenario, two Finnish parents mentioned the concept of consequences; however, the concept was tied to sexual consequences (i.e., pregnancy, sexually transmitted diseases (STDs), or being ready). Neither the Finnish nor the American parents made mention of long-term plans as did the Costa Rican parents (i.e., future marriage plans, educational goals, or career objectives).

COSTA RICAN PARENT: You know, it's very serious. You should think a little before you start doing these things—you should get married first and learn to be responsible! You should think about your studies and not spoil the life of a young girl.

COSTA RICAN PARENT: You have a future, dreams, and a career to go for, don't spoil it. I know you're young, but you have to learn to wait!

FINNISH PARENT: I do not want you to be misused. I hope you are responsible enough to not let this happen at any level.

An apologetic approach was utilized in a variety of ways across the cultural groups. The Costa Rican daughter role was portrayed as the most apologetic for being caught in this difficult situation (53 percent) with six of the eight daughters apologizing before the parent did so. In contrast, only three Costa Rican parents apologized for the interruption and only one initiated the apology. American youths were apologetic, but to a lesser extent (39 percent), while the American parents did not use this approach in any conversation. The Finnish youths were least likely to use an apologetic approach (three Finnish youths). On the other hand, the Finnish parents were largely apologetic for the interruption and embarrassment to their daughters (48 percent) and eleven Finnish parents apologized to their daughters first.

COSTA RICAN PARENT: Sorry Elena, we had problems with our car and I didn't think I'd find you in such a situation. I'm going to be right back, then we'll talk about this.

COSTA RICAN DAUGHTER: Mommy, I'm so sorry, I know you trust me. Oh I'm so embarrassed and I don't know what to say. I'm sorry mommy. I swear it won't happen again, please forgive me!

FINNISH PARENT: Oh, I'm sorry to disturb you, but we had to come home as the car broke down. I guess that you might want to put your clothes back on, so I'll go to another room.

FINNISH DAUGHTER: I am sorry. I'll never do it again and it was really nothing. We haven't done anything, so don't get upset with me.

AMERICAN DAUGHTER: I'm sorry, I know I shouldn't have had him over when you weren't home. I guess we got carried away, I'm sorry.

An approach that was not utilized across groups was an angry and threatening approach. The American parental respondents utilized this approach in a moderate way (17 percent angry, 20 percent threatening) and were the only parents to enter into conversations in this manner. In response, the daughters' reactions ranged from defensive, apologetic, and confrontational. The American daughter respondents were more likely to engage in angry discourse with a high level of denial, as compared to the Finnish daughter respondents who engaged in more rational conversations in which parents and daughters alike were apologetic in their roles and more open to immediate discussion about the situation with the boyfriend present.

AMERICAN PARENT: What is going on here? Just you wait until your father comes in!

AMERICAN PARENT: What is going on here! Both of you get up and get dressed, this is unacceptable!

AMERICAN PARENT: Kim, get your clothes on now! I want the two of you to come out here and talk to me this instant!

AMERICAN DAUGHTER: Oh my God, Mom! What are you doing home? This isn't what it looks like!

AMERICAN DAUGHTER: What are you doing home? You're not supposed to be here—we weren't doing anything, I know what I am doing—if he has to leave, so will I!

Consistent with this approach, American parents were more likely to demand that the boy in the situation leave the house immediately, while fewer Finnish and Costa Rican parents wanted the boy to leave. Over half of the Finnish parents wanted to discuss the situation immediately and while four wanted the boy to stay, four wished him to leave in order to speak with their daughters alone. Costa Rican parents also wanted to discuss the situation immediately (40 percent). Whereas two parents asked the boys to specifically leave, two parents requested them to stay while discussing the situation at length. One American parent requested that the boy stay for further discussion. Other parents chose to delay conversation instead of addressing the issues immediately, although fewer chose this approach. Three Finnish parents wanted to delay further discussion until the next day, whereas two American parents made this request, and only one Costa Rican parent believed it best to save the discussion for a later date. Interestingly, only three American parents in the total sample of sixty-one parents commented that they would contact the boy's parents concerning the situation with their daughters.

Another common theme was age, either that the daughter was too young or that the daughters believed themselves old enough to be participating in such behaviors. Almost half of the Costa Rican parents (47 percent) emphasized that the daughters were too young to be acting in the manner in which they were caught and no daughters disagreed. In comparison, fewer of the Finnish parental respondents stated that the daughters were too young (39 percent) whereas 26 percent of the daughters disagreed and believed themselves old enough. Finally, one American parental respondent brought this topic into the conversation while two American youth mentioned that they believed themselves old enough. Consistent with such findings, disappointment in the daughters was expressed by most of the Costa Rican parental respondents (47 percent) whereas only two Finnish respondents in parental roles and one American parental respondent expressed disappointment.

COSTA RICAN PARENT: According to Costa Rican culture we expect that the situation doesn't happen to a very young girl. However, as a parent I would face this situation telling them that I don't expect that behavior from them. I also will ask if they know the consequences.

FINNISH PARENT: I trusted you Sari. I wouldn't have expected to find you in this situation. You are too young!

FINNISH DAUGHTER: There's nothing for you to decide! I make my own decisions, I'm going to my room to pack, I'm moving out! I'm not a child anymore; I'm old enough.

AMERICAN PARENT: This is the wrong time and place! You are fourteen and still a baby – there is plenty of time for you to share these feelings when you are of age. I can't believe you've done this to me. What on earth were you thinking?

AMERICAN DAUGHTER: My plans were that you wouldn't find out and I am very mature for a fourteen-year-old. It's not like Steve is a child anyway. I mean, he's seventeen and plenty old enough to know what he is doing.

The major theme related to parenting across cultural groups was the relationship between one parent catching the teenagers and then deciding what to do about informing the other parent. Consistent with previous research, less than 20 percent of Costa Rican females communicated with their fathers on topics of sexuality (Schifter & Madrigal, 2000). In the current sample, Costa Rican daughter respondents were also likely to ask their mothers not to share the information about their behavior with their fathers (20 percent). Two Finnish daughters made this request whereas four American daughter respondents asked their mothers not to share the information with the fathers who would soon be entering the living room.

COSTA RICAN DAUGHTER: Please don't growl at me. I'm not doing it anymore, please excuse me! Carlos is going right now, no problem, and don't say anything to dad, please! He'll kill me!

FINNISH DAUGHTER: Mum, what are you doing here? Don't tell daddy, please! We were just sitting there, we didn't do anything.

AMERICAN DAUGHTER: Mother I am so sorry, please forgive me. Please don't tell daddy. He will kill me! Mother, I will explain, I will make it up to you. Please, please don't tell daddy.

An area of concern was a predominant theme of the threat of violence that was portrayed in the U.S. data. Both the parent and daughter mentioned potential violence by the father. Only one Finnish parent mentioned violence although its form was less intimidating.

FINNISH PARENT: I'll kick that boy out of my house and my wife and I will have a little family meeting.

AMERICAN PARENT: You better be sorry. Steve, get out of here before my husband kills you.

AMERICAN DAUGHTER: Are you going to hurt Steve? Please don't it's not his fault, I called him over to the house.

AMERICAN DAUGHTER: Daddy, I'm sorry, please don't beat me.

Not only did the daughter plead for her father not to hurt her or her boyfriend, but she also responded to the American authoritarian parental style with defiance and sarcasm:

AMERICAN DAUGHTER: What do you care? You don't care about me anyway. I don't want to talk to you. I know what I'm doing; you don't understand anything.

AMERICAN DAUGHTER: It is none of your business what I do! I'm going to do what I want. It's not as bad as it looks.

AMERICAN DAUGHTER: You know, you did things like this when you were my age. There's nothing wrong with it.

Sexuality

The qualitative data analysis highlighted the trend that no Costa Rican respondent in either the parental or daughter role mentioned contraception or expectations surrounding contraceptive use. Although the Costa Rican sample was small in size, these data were similar to the findings of Schifter and Madrigal's (2000) Costa Rican sample that indicated only 25 percent of sexually active males and 16 percent of sexually active females used condoms on a regular basis and that younger women are the least likely of all segments of the population to regularly use condoms.

In comparison, the Finnish respondents in parental and daughter roles were much more likely to discuss issues of contraception. Of the thirteen (30 percent) conversations that included the theme of contraception, eight (35 percent) were initiated by those playing the parent role, whereas five daughters mentioned the topic first. In comparison, no Costa Rican within a parental role discussed contraception and only one daughter mentioned the topic. In the United States, three students in parental roles integrated issues of contraception into the conversations, along with one student in the daughter role. This finding suggests that Finnish students are more open to the discussion of contraceptives and sexuality given that the parents were just as likely to bring up the topic as were the youths.

FINNISH PARENT: Later we'll talk about it, like safe sex, AIDS, pregnancy, and her young age in relation to the risk of pregnancy along with what would she do if she would be pregnant? Much of the nature of the discussion would depend on her knowledge and attitude. I'd like to hear from her what she feels.

FINNISH DAUGHTER: I know from my parents what can happen if one practices unsafe sex. Hence, I don't. So you need not worry, I have all the information about protection. As a matter of fact, we were just playing with each other. We are not in a hurry as I don't want to take any chances for abortion or teenage mothering, so please don't worry. We are responsible.

AMERICAN PARENT: Please get dressed and please tell me you are using protection.

AMERICAN DAUGHTER: We are using protection and you wouldn't have found out if you wouldn't have returned early!

A major theme that prominently emerged from the Costa Rican youth was love. Eight of the fifteen respondents (53 percent) mentioned love and all but one daughter brought the topic into the conversation first. Of this group, most Costa Rican youth and one parent connected the concept of love with a "natural act."

COSTA RICAN PARENT: Daughter, you don't have to cry. I understand that sex is something natural and the only thing that matters is that you do it because you're in love and that you take care of yourself.

COSTA RICAN DAUGHTER: This is normal, this is natural, and we love each other.

Two youths did not make the connection between love and a natural act, but did relate love to sexual interaction.

COSTA RICAN DAUGHTER: Remember, we are in a time when sexual relations are something natural and I don't see anything wrong with it.

COSTA RICAN DAUGHTER: I think that sex is something totally natural and we should live that way.

The love theme was also uncovered less often within the Finnish conversations and with a different intent. Three Finnish parents (13 percent) and three Finnish youths (13 percent) incorporated this theme in conversation but no one tied the theme to a "natural act."

FINNISH PARENT: I think you are too young, but I guess it's your decision. Does this boy love you? You know, the first time is supposed to be very romantic and special.

FINNISH DAUGHTER: We were not doing anything, I love this boy!

FINNISH DAUGHTER: He says he loves me, and I like kissing him, but it's hard to talk about these matters.

Finally, the Americans were the least likely to bring love into the conversations given only four daughters (17 percent) mentioned the topic of love and only one daughter associated love with a "natural act," while the others used the topic in more defensive ways.

AMERICAN DAUGHTER: We are in love and lovemaking is a natural thing.

AMERICAN DAUGHTER: I'm sorry, Mom. I love him and we weren't doing anything but laying next to each other naked. I promise.

AMERICAN DAUGHTER: Mom, please don't be irrational. I can explain, just calm down. I love him.

AMERICAN DAUGHTER: I was thinking I was in love and I deserved to have some pleasure in my life.

A theme that is often expected to emerge in teen conversations is peer pressure. This is a chief concern for many teens, as well as parents, because peer pressure is associated with such issues as substance abuse, reckless driving, sex, and a lot of other issues. On the other hand, peer pressure can also be associated with positive teen behaviors such as abstaining from careless sexual involvement or participating in extracurricular school activities. The topic of peer pressure was identified in each culture while the American youths mentioned peer pressure slightly more often than the other two groups (35 percent, as compared to Costa Rica 33 percent, and Finland 23 percent).

In the conversations, American youths were more likely to explain that "everyone is doing it" or "you know you did stuff like this when you were my age" as compared to the other two groups and American youths were more likely to use comments related to "getting carried away."

COSTA RICAN DAUGHTER: Mother, no one believes in virginity anymore. I am not the only one that does it. Everyone does it!

FINNISH DAUGHTER: What do you mean only fourteen? All my friends do it all the time. I'm an adult and it's not a big deal.

AMERICAN DAUGHTER: I'm sorry for yelling, but what's wrong with being naked? We were just having fun. Everybody does it.

DISCUSSION

The original purpose of this learning experience was to involve college students in an experiential learning activity that would enhance their understanding about parenting, parent-child communications, and communications about sexuality. However, after this circular role-play teaching method was utilized in other countries, the potential for cultural insights became increasingly apparent. Since the original purpose was instructional, there are several research limitations. No demographic data were obtained regarding age, gender, race, or parental status of the students involved in the role-play activities. The majority of the students were young adults and female. Therefore, gathering background information from these subjects would have called attention to the male respondents and their responses. Although we do not know the influence of gender when a male played the role of the daughter, the role of gender in one's responses can be incorporated into the post-experience discussion.

Although the activity was facilitated by the same instructor to students of similar age ranges and in courses of similar topics, the cultural context of the activity changed the focus and nature of the resulting communications. Through the qualitative analyses of role-play conversations in a given scenario, a larger picture of cultural differences emerged from the themes within each cultural group. Respondents from each culture in both roles demonstrated varying levels of expressed values and rules, differences in the parenting approach, levels of comfort in confronting the issue at hand immediately or at a later time, and offered specific communications concerning expectations that shaped either positive or negative sexual messages.

In a national sample of U.S. parents, 54 percent reported never talking with their children about sex, 28 percent stated discussions rarely occurred, and 5 percent had discussions once a year (Warren, 1992). Communication related to issues of sexuality can be uncomfortable for many parents and children alike. However, ensuring that positive communication between parents and children takes place is critical in helping young people establish individual values and be better equipped to make sexually healthy decisions. It was clear from the qualitative analyses of the student responses during a role-play activity that distinct patterns emerged within the cultures.

Although there were more similarities in the data than differences, the differences emerged as an overall snapshot picture of the three distinct cultures. Generally, the Costa Rican respondents portrayed parent-child communications with a conservative approach using a long-term, consequential outlook, future goals, trust, love, and responsibility. The Finnish respondents came together to construct a framework of parent-child communications in a more understanding and accepting manner that included discussions of contraception. In contrast, American respondents showed an authoritarian tone in their parent-child communications in which they mentioned respecting authority, responsibility, and peer socialization. Their communications also hinted at the threat of parental violence and concomitant adolescent defiance. However, some of these comments could be cultural colloquialisms and not actual threats of violence. Nevertheless, the level of their anger was apparent. This finding concurs with that of Miller (1998) who found that parental control can be associated with negative effects if it is excessive or coercive.

The bi-directionality of parent-child communications and the escalating symmetry of these interactions are indicative of some of the problems American parents face with adolescents. Teens, whose parents are warm, firm, and grant them psychological autonomy, achieve more in school, report less depression and anxiety, and score higher on measures of self-reliance and self-esteem than teens whose parents fail to demonstrate these key elements in communication (Steinberg, 2001). Furthermore, young people who report feeling a lack of parental warmth, love, or caring were also more likely to report emotional distress, lower self-esteem, drug use, and sexually-risky behaviors (Resnick, et. al, 1997; Steinberg, 2001). Such findings suggest that the authoritarian American parenting approach may be sending a message that values sternness, but disregards teens' abilities to make decisions for themselves. The consequences may result in teens going down destructive paths. Using a "top-down" communication style denies teens the opportunity to discuss their own thoughts, feelings, and desires or to draw links between their own and their parents' perspectives (Yowell, 1997).

Although the activity was utilized as a learning experience in a family relations/human development course, the addition of the cross-cultural data caused a stunned reaction among the students and resulted in some meaningful insights regarding the role of culture in our lives. Cross-cultural comparisons can empower educators and others in professional settings to create a broader understanding of cultural influences in our views of parenting, communication styles, and sexuality.

This activity can also be used to highlight ethnocentric issues, as well as cultural differences that may help facilitate an ethnorelative perspective. With the support of cross-cultural data, this activity can encourage students to exercise their critical thinking skills about their own cultural beliefs and values, to ask questions that help them build a more culturally sensitive perspective, and to facilitate deeper understandings and meanings surrounding the complexities of parenting and sexuality both individually and broadly.

As family life educators in higher education set new goals, take risks, form new relationships, and discover the potential of diversity, they are blazing trails that are not always easy to follow. Educators should accept a role in transforming the profession and society by taking specific actions and tapping the possibilities within our own life contexts.

The experiences and insights of the participants in this study provide a number of implications for the field of family life education. Educators and students in university programs can enhance personal understanding by reading novels, essays, and biographies written by authors from a variety of cultural backgrounds, as well as engaging in shared learning experiences with students from other cultures. Professors should each reflect on personal experiences regarding how their families portrayed others from different backgrounds, how their friends talked about and treated others, and how their own personal strengths and biases may influence their perceptions of families and persons from other cultures. They can draw on their own histories to assess abilities, skills, and areas for further growth.

Similarly, university instructors in selected courses should require students to reflect upon and write about past and recent experiences in which adventures in other cultures played a role and how they can build skills and values to prepare for work in a diverse society. Furthermore, curriculum and program development should be altered to be more inclusive of a multicultural perspective. According to Banks (1994), a transformation approach to multicultural education can alter the structure, assumptions, and perspectives of the curricula so that subject matter can be viewed from the perspectives and experiences of a range of groups. If Americans want to become more internationally savvy, our parochial cultural beliefs need to be questioned.

University programs and other professional groups should support travel to other cultures, either to other parts of the world or to various neighborhoods within a city, state, or country. Whenever possible, teaching, studying, and working in diverse settings would provide valuable insights to all those concerned. Students and professionals should become directly involved with short- and long-term professional projects or service/learning assignments in which they interact with people unlike themselves.

Research must continue regarding a wide variety of diversity issues. Phenomenological studies are needed to investigate how people from varied backgrounds perceive the meanings related to family functioning and the quality of individual and family life. Future interviews and observations should be conducted among a more culturally and professionally diverse sample of participants than this study. Action research could be especially useful in increasing understanding about the processes, roles, challenges, questions, goals, and outcomes related to other cultures and particular diversity issues within those settings.

As diversity increases in our nation's schools, teachers, administrators, practitioners, and researchers will be increasingly challenged to become more knowledgeable about the assumptions, attributes, and norms of a range of cultures. These challenges will occur in every dimension of the educational system and although the issue of cross-cultural perspectives and diversity are complex, those working with students can incorporate activities that facilitate cultural learning in a variety of ways.

This particular teaching activity is not complicated, but an abundance of rich information can be gathered and learned from each use of the activity, regardless of the cultural setting. Utilizing this activity can be a nonthreatening strategy to introduce students to ideas of diversity and of perspectives that may differ from their own. Incorporating activities that support diversity in our classrooms is a necessity in a world that is quickly becoming smaller due to technology and increasing involvement in a global market. Since preparing our students to enter this changing society is crucial, it is our charge to expand their horizons and ensure that they are prepared to be effective members of the global community.

REFERENCES

Alzate, H. (1984). Sexual behavior of unmarried Colombian university students: A five-year follow up. *Archives of Sexual Behavior, 13,* 121-132.

Banks, J. (1994). Transforming the mainstream curriculum. *Journal of the Association for Supervision and Curriculum Development, 51,* 4-8.

Blackwood, E. (2000). Culture and women's sexualities. *Journal of Social Issues, 56,* 223-238.

Bogdan, R. & Biklen, S. (1992). *Qualitative research for education.* Boston: Allyn and Bacon.

Brown, J. (2002). Mass media influences on sexuality. *The Journal of Sex Research, 39,* 42-45.

Buss, D. (1989). Sex differences in human mate preferences: Evolutionary hypotheses tested in 37 countries. *Behavioral and Brain Sciences, 12,* 1-49.

Centers for Disease Control and Prevention (2000). Youth risk behavior surveillance—United States. *Morbidity and Morality Weekly Report, 49,* SS-5.

Christensen, H. (1973). Attitudes toward marital infidelity: A nine-cultural sampling of university student opinion. *Journal of Comparative Family Studies, 4,* 197-214.

Cochran, S., Mays, V., & Leung, L. (1991). Sexual practices of heterosexual Asian American young adults: Implications for risk of HIV infection. *Archives of Sexual Behavior, 20,* 381-392.

Comas-Diaz, L. (1987). Feminist therapy with mainland Puerto Rican women. *Psychology of Women Quarterly, 11,* 461-474.

Cresswell, J. (1998). *Qualitative inquiry and research design: Choosing from among five traditions.* Newbury Park, CA: Sage Publications.

Cresswell, J. (2003). *Research design: Qualitative, quantitative, and mixed methods approaches.* Newbury Park, CA: Sage Publications.

Darling, C., Haavio-Mannila, E., & Kontula, O. (2001). Understanding orgasmic frequency: A case of Finland. *Scandinavian Journal of Sexology* (formerly *Nordic Sexologi), 4,* 89-106.

Darling, C. & Hollon, S. (2002) Human sexuality. In D. Bredehoft & M. Walcheski (Eds.), *Family life education: Integrating theory and practice* (pp. 82-91). Minneapolis, MN: National Council on Family Relations.

Denzin, N. & Lincoln, Y. (1994). *Handbook of qualitative research.* Thousand Oaks, CA: Sage Publications.

Denzin. N. & Lincoln, Y. (1998a). *Collecting and interpreting qualitative materials.* Thousand Oaks, CA: Sage Publications.

Denzin, N. & Lincoln, Y. (1998b). *Strategies of qualitative inquiry.* Thousand Oaks, CA: Sage Publications.

Gardiner, H., Mutter, J., & Kosmitzki, C. (1998). *Lives across cultures: Cross-cultural human development.* Needham Heights, MA: Allyn and Bacon.

Hogan, D. & Kitagawa, E. (1985). The impact of social status, family structure, and neighborhood on the fertility of Black adolescents. *American Journal of Sociology, 90,* 825-855.

Hutchinson, M. & Cooney, T. (1998). Patterns of parent-teen sexual risk communication: Implications for intervention. *Family Relationships, 47,* 185-194.

Iwawaki, S. & Eysenck, H. (1978). Sexual attitudes among British and Japanese students. *Journal of Psychology, 98,* 289-298.

Jaccard, J., Dittus, P., & Gordon, V. (1996). Maternal correlates of adolescent sexual and contraceptive behavior. *Family Planning Perspectives, 28,* 159-165.

Janesick, V. (1994). The dance of qualitative research design: Metaphor, methodolatry, and meaning. In N. Denzin & Y. Lincoln (Eds.), *Handbook of qualitative research* (pp. 209-220). Thousand Oaks, CA: Sage Publications.

Joyner, K. & Laumann, E. (2001). Teenage sex and the sexual evolution. In E.O. Laumann & R.T. Michael (Eds.), *Sex, love and health in America: Private choices and public policies* (pp. 41-71). Chicago: University of Chicago Press.

Kontula, O. & Haavio-Mannila, E. (1995). *Sexual pleasures: Enhancement of sex life in Finland, 1971-1992.* Brookfield, VT: Dartmouth Publishing.

Kunkel, D., Cope, S., Farinola, W., Biely, E., Rollin, E., & Donnerstein, E. (1999). Sex on TV: A biennial report to the Kaiser Family Foundation, 1999. Menlo Park, CA: The Henry Kaiser Family Foundation.

LaBeff, E. & Dodder, R. (1982). Attitudes toward sexual permissiveness in Mexico and the United States. *The Journal of Social Psychology, 116,* 285-286.

Luster, T. & Small, S. (1997). Sexual abuse history and number of sex partners among female adolescents. *Family Planning Perspectives, 29,* 204-211.

McCann, F. & Petrich-Kelly, B. (1999). Learning to feel good about yourself: Public education reconsidered. *SIECUS Report, 27,* 24-27.

Miles, M. & Huberman, M. (1994). *Qualitative data analysis.* Newbury Park, CA: Sage Publications.

Miller, B. (1998). *Families matter: A research synthesis of family influences of adolescent pregnancy.* Washington, DC: National Campaign to Prevent Teen Pregnancy.

Miller, B. (2002). Family influences on adolescent sexual contraceptive behavior. *The Journal of Sex Research, 39,* 22-26.

Miller, B., Benson, B., & Galbraith, K. (2001). 10 family relationships and adolescent pregnancy risks: A research synthesis. *Developmental Review, 21,* 1-38.

Miller, B., Norton, M., Fan, X., & Christopherson, C. (1998). Pubertal development, parental communication, and sexual values in relation to adolescent sexual behavior. *The Journal of Early Adolescence, 18,* 27-52.

Miller, W., Pasta, D., MacMurray, J., Chiu, C., Wu, H., & Comings, D. (1999). Dopamine receptor genes are associated with age at first sexual intercourse. *Journal of Biosocial Science, 31,* 43-54.

Ojanlatva, A., Helenius, H., Rautava, P., Ahvenainen, J., Koskenvuo, M. (2003). Importance of and satisfaction with sex life in a large Finnish population. *Sex Roles, 48,* 543-553.

Patton, M. (2002). *Qualitative research and evaluation methods.* Thousand Oaks, CA: Sage.

Raffaelli, M. & Green, S. (2003). Parent-adolescent communication about sex: Retrospective reports by Latino college students. *Journal of Marriage and Family, 65,* 474-481.

Remez, L. (2000). Oral sex among adolescents: Is it sex or is it abstinence? *Family Planning Perspectives, 32,* 298-304.

Resnick, M., Bearman, P., Blum, R., Badman, K., Harris, K., Jones, J., et al. (1997). Protecting adolescents from harm: Findings from the National Longitudinal Study on Adolescent Health. *Journal of American Medical Association, 278,* 823-832.

Schifter, J. & Madrigal, J. (2000). *The sexual construction of Latino youth: Implications for the spread of HIV/AIDS.* Binghamton, NY: The Haworth Hispanic/Latino Press.

Shapurian, R. & Hojat, M. (1985). Sexual and premarital attitudes of Iranian college students. *Psychological Reports, 57,* 67-74.

Steinberg, L. (2001). We know some things: Parent-adolescent relationships in retrospect and prospect. *Journal of Research on Adolescence, 5,* 31-53.

Strauss, A. & Corbin, J. (1990). *Basics of qualitative research: Grounded theory procedures and techniques.* Newbury Park, CA: Sage Publications.

Taipale, V. (Ed.) (1995). Women: The pillars of society. In *Finland: How to become a Finn* (pp. 36-37). Helsinki, Finland: Yleisradion Oy.

Trussell, J. & Vaughn, B. (1991). *Selected results concerning sexual behavior and contraceptive use from the 1988 National Survey of Family Growth and the 1988 National Survey of Adolescent Males* (Working Paper 91-12). Princeton, NJ: Office of Population Research.

Upchurch, D., Aneshensel, C., Sucoff, C., & Levy-Storms, L. (1999). Neighbor-hood and family contexts of adolescent sexual activity. *Journal of Marriage and the Family, 61,* 920-933.

Warren, C. (1992). Perspectives on international sex practices and American family sex communication relevant to teenage sexual behavior in the United States. *Health Communication, 4,* 121-136.

Werebe, M. & Reinert, M. (1983). Attitudes of French adolescents toward sexual-ity. *Journal of Adolescence, 6,* 145-159.

Yowell, C. (1997). Risks of communication: Early adolescent girls' conversations with mothers and friends about sexuality. *Journal of Early Adolescence, 17,* 172-196.

Chapter 3

How Big Is the Penguin?
Designing and Teaching a Course in
Comparative Family Policy

Steven K. Wisensale

How many of us remember those *National Geographic* film clips showing penguins grouped together on an ice flow in Antarctica? Because there was usually no means for comparing the size of the penguins to other beings or objects familiar to us, we often convinced ourselves that they must have been at least six feet tall. It was only after we witnessed a human being walking among the penguins (for me that did not occur until my early teens) that we had some degree of perspective and could better compare the size of penguins to other objects. "How big is the penguin?" is the first question I pose on the very first day of my comparative family policy course. I first place a photo of a penguin on the screen, followed by a picture of several penguins, some smaller, some larger than others. "How big is the penguin?" I ask. The answer is still elusive for students who are struggling for a comparative reference point. However, when I slide a picture of an SUV onto the screen next to a penguin, followed by a photo of Michael Jordan, who is six feet-nine inches tall, a more precise comparison can be made and the size of the penguins can be better approximated.

As we move into a new century, one of the most encouraging developments in higher education in particular is a growing emphasis on diversity in course offerings and their content. Emphasized less, but equally important (particularly since 9/11) is the internationalization

doi:10.1300/5609_03

49

of the curricula. Although comparative studies are well entrenched in such disciplines as political science and anthropology, the same cannot be said for family studies curricula in general and family policy in particular. In short, our students need to know more about the world, the families that live there, and the variety of policies that affect those families. In doing so, by comparing U.S. family policy to policies in other countries ("How big is the penguin?"), they will get a better and more realistic international perspective on families that will make them more enlightened students, effective practitioners, and better-informed citizens. As they emerge from a sheltered and often isolated campus and enter a complex and often intimidating world, the question of "Compared to what?" should become a major reference point on their intellectual compasses. Although the difficulties in teaching comparative studies have been well documented by Cox (1993), Clignet (1991), and Larson (1980), one means for achieving this goal is to offer a course on comparative family policy.

In 2004 the United Nations marked the Tenth Anniversary of the International Year of the Family (IYF). This chapter discusses ten years of experience in teaching a course in comparative family policy. What follows is my reflection on designing and teaching this course from an international perspective. Discussed is the academic setting within which the course is taught, the objectives of the course and its contents, examples of classroom exercises created and utilized, learning materials employed, term projects assigned, and various options for evaluating students progress. The chapter will conclude with suggestions and guidelines for designing a similar course.

THE ACADEMIC SETTING

The School of Family Studies at the University of Connecticut consists of about twenty full-time tenured or tenure-track professors and another twenty adjuncts. Approximately 500 undergraduate students and between 75 and 100 graduate students attend at any given time (depending on their progress in completing master's theses and doctoral dissertations). The undergraduate curriculum is divided into four major components, from which students select a particular concentration. These include childhood and adolescence, adulthood and aging, counseling, and social policy and planning. Most students are white females who were born and raised in homogeneous suburban

Connecticut communities and entered the university directly from high school. Only a small number have traveled abroad and relatively few have participated in the University's study-abroad program. Equally significant, according to a recent survey, about 76 percent of family studies students have never taken a course in political science. In short, most students in the course are upperclassmen who have had little exposure to international affairs. Both their backgrounds and interests in American politics, let alone international politics, are extremely limited. Although there is no prerequisite for the course, students are encouraged to take a public policy and family course that is offered in the preceding fall term.

Faculty who teach in urban settings and/or have a more diverse student body should consider the various ways that diversity, both within the classroom and in the city, can be utilized in the teaching and learning process. For example, personal stories from students about their families' immigration experiences, foreign films, and the voting patterns among ethnic groups within an urban setting could all serve as discussion "icebreakers" early in the course and during future class meetings.

OBJECTIVES AND COURSE CONTENT

Over the eleven years that the course has been offered, the objectives have remained remarkably the same with only minor changes. The course content, however, has changed considerably, as it should if one is dedicated to keeping pace with family issues on an international scale. The five major objectives of the course are presented as follows.

1. To develop an analytical framework in comparative policy analysis that can be applied to family policy in particular
2. To effectively compare U.S. family policy to family policies in other countries according to distinct categories
3. To identify specific strengths and weaknesses of family policies in the United States and other countries
4. To understand why differences exist between family policy in the United States compared to other countries

5. To produce and consider particular policy recommendations that may benefit America's families

In terms of content, the course is divided into seven major segments, with about two weeks allocated for each topic. First, the introduction to the course consists of a series of in-class exercises (to be described later in this chapter) combined with a series of carefully selected readings on comparative policy analysis. Included are Zimmerman's (1992) "Political Culture: Definitions and Variations in 50 States," Jansson's (2001) "Why Has the American Welfare State Been Reluctant?" and Wisensale's (2001) "The Family and American Politics." The purpose is threefold: to expose students to cultural differences within their own country, to give them a firm foundation for understanding American family policy, and to offer them at least one explanation for why the United States has a reputation for being a reluctant welfare state.

The second segment is devoted to demographics and the changing family worldwide. Included are journal readings and Web site documents that explore the reasons for lower fertility in industrialized societies compared to extremely high birth rates in many developing nations. Case studies of coercive family planning policies include China's one-child policy, the Romanian orphanage disasters, and female infanticide in parts of India. These examples are compared to more collaborative efforts at birth control, as illustrated by the two-child policy initiatives in Egypt and Vietnam and the Indian state of Kerala's approach that has maintained a stable demographic profile for more than a century. Clearly, population policies affect family well-being and, in the case of industrialized countries where lower fertility coexists with an aging population, long-established social welfare systems are being challenged. Will there be enough young people to not only support the traditional pay-as-you-go pension programs but will there be enough informal caregivers available? This latter phenomenon, which is a relatively recent development, will also affect the general health and well-being of the world's families.

Segment three focuses on the care of children. Most of the readings and Web site assignments are devoted to child care policies in developed nations. Comparisons among the European Union countries and the United States with respect to child care are made easier by visiting The Clearinghouse on International Developments in Child, Youth and Family Policies, available at its Web site (http://www.childpolicy intl.org). Although as many as twenty countries can be compared, it is perhaps better to limit the options to six or seven selected countries.

In an effort to create a lifespan framework for analyzing the world's families, the fourth segment concentrates on worldwide youth issues. Covered in this segment are the issues of teen pregnancy (why does the United States have the highest rate and the Netherlands the lowest?), child labor, child soldiers, and the United Nations Convention on the Rights of the Child. Most of the readings for this portion of the course are available on the Web. Raising the question as to why the United States is only one of two countries (Somalia is the other) that has not ratified the International Rights of the Child is guaranteed to ignite a lively discussion. Similarly, raising the question about the manufacturing source for much of the clothing sold in university co-ops should spark student interest in child labor and sweat-shops abroad, as well as encourage them to be more thoughtful about their purchases in the future: Where was my college sweatshirt produced and by whom?

Since 1994, and the celebration of the International Year of Older Persons in 1999, more attention has been devoted to world population aging. Recognizing this, segment five of the course explores the ramifications of global aging for families in particular. Again, most of the readings are Web based and confined to industrialized societies, but aging in developing countries, often overlooked by researchers and the media, is also covered. In both cases students are required to draw their attention to the question of allocating resources across generations fairly and to the issue of intergenerational equity. How societies address the needs of their aging citizens compared to dependent children will surely affect families, both emotionally and economically.

Segment six examines work and family conflict from an international perspective. Particularly among developed countries, comparisons can be made in terms of the percentage of mothers in the workforce, how many work full-time versus part-time, male wages compared to female wages, and the various models of parental leave available to families. What is the length of leave and its wage replacement by country? This topic can also be explored in developing nations. Children are often removed from school prematurely to work and help support their families. Policies and programs offer alternatives to this approach. Appropriate readings and Web site assignments for covering this topic are accessible and should be assigned.

The final portion of the course concentrates on family law and women's rights. Following a general lecture on marriage law and divorce rates worldwide, much attention is devoted to gender equity and women's rights, particularly in developing countries. For example, genital mutilation, honor killings, and blood feuds are discussed within the context of human rights. Also covered is marriage reform in Vietnam (primarily because the author completed a study tour there and published several papers on the topic). Following the completion of this component, the course concludes with a review of what had been covered throughout the term, how the United States compares to other countries in family policy, and what the future may hold for families in developed and developing countries.

CLASSROOM EXERCISES

Following the opening exercise (How big is the penguin?), the importance of establishing a clear perspective prior to doing comparative analysis is strongly emphasized. This brief introduction to the course on the first day of class is followed by another exercise, a series of questions that probe the students' knowledge of world demographics. For example, if we could shrink the world to 100 people, how many would be Asians, Europeans, Africans, white or nonwhite, Christian or non-Christian, wealthy or poor, literate or illiterate, well-fed or malnourished? Students are asked to write down their responses and compare them to the correct answers that are placed on the screen for review and further discussion. An example of this exercise appears as follows (Smith & Armstrong, 2002).

If We Could Shrink the World to 100 People

57 would be Asians
21 would be Europeans
14 would come from the Western Hemisphere
 8 would be Africans
70 would be nonwhite, 30 would be white
70 would be non Christian, 30 Christian
50 percent of world's wealth would be controlled by 6 people

All 6 people would be citizens of the United States
70 people cannot read and only one has a college degree
50 would suffer from malnutrition

A course in comparative family policy lends itself to the creation and utilization of case studies. Some can even be lifted from the front pages of daily newspapers. For example, several years ago a couple left their infant alone in a baby carriage outside a New York restaurant. Concerned citizens notified the police about the "abandoned" baby and the couple was arrested for negligence and they lost custody of their child for several weeks. The unknown here is that the "negligent" couple was from Denmark where placing a child alone in a carriage on the street is quite common and does not violate the law. As a graduate student in Sweden, I can recall walking the streets of Stockholm and noticing many babies in carriages parked unattended outside apartment buildings in the dead of winter. To bring this example of a culture clash to light a short case is presented as follows.

The Unattended Baby

Assume that you and your friends decide to spend the day in New York City. You arrive by train around 12:00 noon and head directly for a restaurant that was recommended by a friend. Just as you are entering the restaurant, you notice that there is an unattended baby in a carriage parked on the sidewalk in front of the restaurant. Upon entering the restaurant you notice, from inside the restaurant (although there are a few windows) the baby carriage is no longer visible.

Questions

1. Are you concerned about the unattended infant? Or, is it someone else's problem?
2. If you are concerned, what would you do, if anything? Tell the manager? Call the police? Shout out loud across the restaurant that there is an unattended baby outside?
3. Would you assume the parents are either eating or working in the restaurant?

4. If the parents are in the restaurant and they identify themselves, what would you do or say, if anything, to them?
5. Would you view the parent or parents' action here as neglect? Abuse? If you feel strongly that the parents are neglectful or abusive, what would you recommend be done to them?

Following a class discussion that is focused on the questions, students are informed that the couple is from Denmark where the custom is to leave babies unattended in public places. Because it probably is not a wise idea to leave your baby alone in New York City, the couple needs to be made aware of the dangers of doing so. It is also important for students to learn that cultures and customs differ across nations and they frequently come into conflict. Recently, a Muslim woman in Florida refused to remove her veil for her driver's license photo. The case went to court. Similarly, a Vietnamese couple in Los Angeles was arrested for child abuse when it appeared that one of their children had large red welts on the back and stomach. An investigation revealed, however, that the red spots were caused by "coining," a common, homegrown medical practice in some Asian countries in which coins are heated in oil and then rubbed on an ill person's body in a circular motion. This procedure creates large red spots that look like welts.

Many other classroom exercises can be created and used to inform students about different cultures and customs. For example, should African women who seek to avoid genital mutilation be given political asylum in the United States? What are the rights of a divorced parent in the United States whose children are abducted by an ex-spouse and taken to a foreign country where permanent custody without visitation is granted to the abductor? What should be the role of international organizations that are aware of honor killings, blood feuds, and other examples of intimate violence against women? A variety of hypothetical cases can be created and used for class discussions.

Morrison, Conaway, and Borden's (1994) *Kiss, Bow or Shake Hands: How to Do Business in Sixty Countries* provides information and exposure to customs in different countries. By assigning one country per student (chapters are only three or four pages in length) and then arranging for each student to meet their fellow students representing two other countries in which they describe their particular customs, much can be learned in a fairly efficient way. Similarly, Ahn and Gilbert's (1992) journal article, "Cultural Diversity and Sexual Abuse Prevention," can be used for case material to help stimulate class discussion. For example, in some cultures, family bathing is quite common and continues when immigrants arrive in America. Also, in some cultures, it is acceptable for young children to sleep with parents. How should American social workers deal with such situations? These are the types of questions that are currently being asked and to which our students should be exposed prior to beginning their careers in human services, in which they will be confronted with many diverse cultures and customs.

Even though the focus is on comparative family policy and the class exercises may be effective, another option for introducing the subject matter is to expose students to cultural differences within the United States. Shirley Zimmerman's (1992), "Political Culture: Definitions and Variations in 50 States" is one tool for achieving this objective. Building on Daniel Elazar's (1984) work on political culture, Zimmerman separates proactive "family-friendly" states from states that prefer little government intervention in family matters. For example, Minnesota is far more aggressive legislatively in addressing family issues compared to Nevada and South Carolina. (Because many of my students come from New England, I point out the glaring differences in political culture between Vermont and New Hampshire, which not only border each other but are within a short drive of the University of Connecticut, a state that has its own unique political culture.) Zimmerman's work provides a good reference point for future class discussions when explanations for differences between countries in family policy are called for. Political culture is a powerful force.

THE SELECTION AND USE
OF LEARNING MATERIALS

For the past ten years most of the learning materials selected for this course have consisted of books, journal articles, case studies, Web site assignments, and carefully selected videos. With respect to the selection of books, one is limited by whether or not the available material is current. World events and family policies change daily, it is important to constantly evaluate the relevance of the reading material being assigned. For example, without question, the classic in the field of comparative family policy is Kamerman and Kahn's (1978) *Family Policy: Government and Families in Fourteen Countries,* but it is now more than twenty-five years old. Another classic is Alva and Gunnar Myrdal's (1934) *The Nation and the Family: Crisis in the Population Question.* However, although such works may not be suitable for required reading today, each book contains informative chapters that remain relevant—such as descriptions of methodologies employed and helpful tools for conducting research across nations and cultures.

Resources

Other helpful resources include Norman Ginsburg's (1992) *Divisions of Welfare: A Critical Introduction to Comparative Social Policy;* Maureen Baker's (1995) *Canadian Family Policies: Cross-National Comparisons;* Anne Helene Gauthier's (1996) *The State and the Family: A Comparative Analysis of Family Policies in Industrialized Countries;* and Kathy O'Hara's (1998) *Comparative Family Policy: Eight Countries' Stories.* Ginsburg's book, now somewhat dated and no longer assigned, provided a broad overview of social welfare policies in six different industrialized countries, including the United States. Baker's work, despite its title, compares eight different countries, including the United States and Canada. O'Hara also focuses on eight countries, including the United States, while Gauthier covers family policy in the United States and twenty European countries.

A more recent book that is currently under consideration for use in the course is Elaine Leeder's (2003) *The Family in Global Perspective.* Although not geared specifically to public policy, Leeder uses various historical, theoretical, and comparative perspectives to develop a cross-cultural understanding of family life. She examines a variety of family lives in Western countries and contrasts them with families in parts of Africa, Asia, and Latin America. If the book is not adopted for classroom use, at least the final chapter ("The Future of the Family in Global Perspective") should be assigned reading in any comparative family studies course. Other recent books worth considering for classroom use include Pfenning and Bahle's (2001) *Families and Family Policies in Europe: Comparative Perspectives;* Kaufman, Kuijsten, Schulze, and Strohmeier's (2002) *Family Life and Family Policies in Europe: Problems and Issues in Comparative Perspective;*

and Rainwater and Smeeding's (2003) *Poor Kids in a Rich Country: America's Children in Comparative Perspective.*

Clearly, a major gap in the literature is the limited coverage of family policies in non-Western societies and/or developing nations. However, this can be corrected through carefully selected readings culled from appropriate journals, shortpaper assignments, major course projects, or required Web site readings. Four web sites in particular are extremely helpful in teaching the course. The Web site of the Clearinghouse on International Developments in Child, Youth and Family Policies (2004) at the School of Social Work at Columbia University, offers updated information on family policies in more than twenty countries. Child care programs, parental-leave policies, youth policies, health and education programs, and family-oriented tax policies are compared across countries. The Vanier Institute of the Family in Canada (2004) also offers a Web site for comparing American and Canadian family policies. The Web site of the Australian Institute of Family Studies (2004) provides information on more countries and their family policies than perhaps any other site. The United Nations' (Family Unit, 2004) Web site on the family provides information from the 1994 International Year of the Family. Recently, the United Nations created a new independent news service that covers topics such as women and children. The UN Wire (2004) can be accessed easily and both instructors and students can subscribe to a LISTSERV that provides regular updates on international affairs, including family matters.

Other course resources include assigned readings (journal articles and book chapters), which are scanned by the library and posted on electronic course reserve, and videos, many of which are taped from TV specials. Guest speakers, who often are foreign graduate students or undergraduates who recently returned from a study-abroad program can be invited to describe family life in their respective countries. Also, because the University of Connecticut has funded a major human rights initiative on campus, many outstanding figures from around the world are invited to campus for major lectures and special seminars. Depending on the speaker or topic and how it relates to the course content, students may be assigned to attend the lecture, take notes, and come to class prepared to discuss the major points that were raised. Yet of all the approaches described, bringing in foreign graduate students to discuss their family life is perhaps the most stimulating exercise. Not only are the foreign students encouraged to talk about family customs in their countries, they are also asked to provide observations of customs and habits of American young people in their age range. Finally, not to be overlooked are films shown on campus (or off) that coincide with the objectives of the course. These too can be assigned and serve as catalysts for class discussions.

COURSE PROJECTS

The assignment of class projects varies from term to term, but usually students are required to maintain a "current events" clip file that includes international news coverage of matters relevant to the course. A session is set aside at least once a week in which students are invited to share their news items with the class. A total of fifteen articles (one a week) is required to be collected and placed in some sort of binder to be turned in at the conclusion of the semester. Summaries of TV news stories or documentaries are also acceptable.

A major project or paper is always required for the course. This usually takes the form of a twenty-page document or its equivalent in another format. It must include a fairly sophisticated analysis that is related to a family issue and be comparative in structure. This assignment is used primarily to cover topics that were not otherwise addressed in the course. Students select or are assigned a country or two that were not covered in class and, working within a specified framework of guiding questions, gather information and draw conclusions. Because many student projects are never presented in class, due to time limitations, I always set aside at least one class period in which students are divided into groups of four in which they share their papers with one another during fifteen-minute time slots. By rotating them through the various groups four times (one hour in all), students make four presentations of their work to their classmates but also hear twelve different reports on other countries. Also, each student must prepare a one-page abstract that will be distributed to all of his or her classmates so that everyone in the class shares their knowledge with one another.

GRADING AND EVALUATING STUDENTS

Grading is never a popular topic, but with my classes averaging fifty students per term, I find that fairness in weighing course work is always the best policy. Therefore, because discussions are encouraged and regular attendance is expected, 20 percent of the final grade is devoted to class participation. Another 20 percent is set aside for the class project and three in-class exams, including the final, count 20 percent each.

When working at a research university, where the demand for publishing papers and acquiring grant funds is great, one is tempted to avoid class projects and give only objective exams. However, even with a relatively large class it is still possible to strike a compromise. A major written assignment is always required. With respect to exams, multiple choice and short-answer questions make up about 40 percent of the exam with the remaining 60 percent consisting of essay questions. However, because the final is a two-hour exam, a different format is employed. Students should be given the opportunity to pull together lots of knowledge acquired during the term. Therefore, the exam often consists of one or two essay questions and, in some cases, sample questions are provided in advance to jump-start students' thinking. Or, a portion of the final may be of the take-home variety. Whatever the case, and regardless if the exam is the final or not, students are usually given a problem to solve in a hypothetical country and are always required to draw comparisons between nations. An excerpt from a previously used essay question is presented as follows.

> Assume that you have been accepted into a summer internship program sponsored by the United Nations. You are dispatched to the Geneva, Switzerland, office for three weeks of intense training before being officially assigned to the country of Shay. You are informed by your training instructor in Geneva that you were selected by Shay because of your interest in comparative family policy. During your three weeks in Geneva you spend most of your time reading selected books and articles on the history, culture, and politics of Shay, as well as learning the language (Shadshay) and gathering new knowledge about its culture and customs. However, upon your arrival in Shay, theory makes room for reality. Within hours of assuming your internship, your supervisor in Shay presents you with your first challenge. In an effort to

learn more about your background and skills, as well as get a better picture of your general understanding of Shay's demographic and social trends, she gives you the following assignment.

What follows are two pages of graphs that include a picture of Shay's demographic pyramid which displays the distribution of its population by age and sex, a graph depicting the nation's fertility rate in comparison to its growing aging population, another graph displaying the teen pregnancy rate, and a final graph that illustrates the rising poverty rate among children in Shay's single-parent households. Students are then asked four questions:

1. What general conclusions can be reached regarding Shay's major demographic trends?
2. Which two demographic trends in particular concern you most and why?
3. With respect to the two demographic trends that concern you most, what are the policy implications associated with these trends? That is, what policies would you suggest be considered by the country of Shay to address these trends?
4. In responding to question 3, which country or countries that we have covered so far in class would be most helpful in serving as a model or models for the specific policies you recommend? Explain.

This represents just one example of an exam question. Many other possibilities exist, including child abuse, rising divorce rates, women entering the labor force, children's rights, marriage reforms, the rights of same-sex partners, and the pros and cons of filial responsibility laws. Whatever is selected, the emphasis should be on both problem solving and comparative analysis within the context of international family policy.

MEASURING PEDAGOGICAL EFFECTIVENESS

Evaluating the academic accomplishments of individual students in a course is one thing, determining the effectiveness of the course as a whole is quite another matter. To achieve this objective, two tools are utilized. First, a pre- and posttest on political and geographical awareness is administered—the former on the second day of the course; the latter on the last day. Specific questions concerning names of political leaders, international issues, current news stories, and the locations and capitals of particular countries are included in the instrument that is given before and after the course content has been absorbed. However, the only thing different on the second test is an open-ended question that asks students to list the most important lessons they learned from the course.

The second instrument used to measure teaching effectiveness is the standard course evaluation form that is required by the university. Students complete the forms at the end of the course, evaluating the instructor on organization, presentation, fairness in grading, stimulating interest, and additional categories. Use this opportunity to ask students to provide their thoughts and comments on the learning materials used during the semester, including books, articles, Web-based reading assignments, and videos. Which materials did students find to be more informative than others? Which items in particular should be evaluated again and perhaps discarded? Based on the feedback gathered from these two instruments, the course is revised accordingly.

SUGGESTIONS AND GUIDELINES

For the past eleven years I have had the opportunity to create and teach a course on comparative family policy. During that period I have learned much from the content matter and the students who enrolled in my course. Following are several points worth considering in designing and offering a similar course.

First, as instructors, we need to constantly remind ourselves to avoid viewing the United States as "normal" or "right" in comparing the policies of other nations to our own. Emphasize that policies are often the product of culture. What may be appropriate for one nation may not work for another. However, we can all share ideas with one another, consider new approaches to solving problems, and learn much in the process.

Second, require each student to bring a map to class and encourage them to refer to it frequently during lectures and class discussions. I found the geographical knowledge of students severely lacking. Placing a map on the screen while discussing specific countries should be common practice. Whatever comments can be made with respect to geopolitics is a plus and much appreciated by students who have traveled little in their young lives.

Third, be patient. Keep in mind that students entering your class probably have very little background in government or public policy and are even more limited in their knowledge about the world in general. Start slow with effective, nonthreatening classroom exercises that encourage students to view the world from an entirely different perspective. How big is the penguin? Compared to what?

Fourth, stay current with the news. The topic is dynamic, fluid, and constantly changing from term to term. Therefore, the syllabus should not and will not become stagnant. Books, articles, and Web sites will change substantially over the years, as they should. That is what makes teaching such a course so stimulating. The challenge of keeping current on family policy worldwide should be embraced, not resisted.

Fifth, technology is your friend. Web site assignments can be extremely effective and help to fill many information gaps that are not captured in the required readings. Specific reading assignments include visits to Web pages of international organizations, perusal of foreign-based English newspapers on the Internet, and frequent references to United Nations documents and nongovernmental organization (NGO) reports that are accessible via the Web. I also use WebCT, which is a university-based software program that allows communication with the entire class, simultaneously, posting of impromptu readings or announcements, and provides a chat room for discussions that can extend beyond the classroom.

Sixth, keep your VCR and DVD players warmed up and a supply of blank tapes or disks nearby. Many programs on TV can be easily taped and shown in class. These include PBS specials, network news reports, and documentaries. I have accumulated a library of such tapes that range from China's one-child policy, to infanticide in India, to international adoption law, to social welfare policy in Norway. Also, some news organizations maintain fairly comprehensive archives of previously covered stories that can be accessed by the students via the Web.

Finally, be imaginative and creative. A short article in the newspaper about an honor killing in Brazil can be converted to a short case for class discussion. Also, become aware of opportunities to travel and study abroad during your free time in the summer. I have participated in three study seminars in the past six years that included trips to Vietnam, the Netherlands, and Germany. For example, the Council of International Education Exchange (2004) offers a dozen or so one- to two-week study tours each summer for faculty members. For those who are really ambitious and interested in spending a semester teaching on a ship as it travels around the world, contact Semester at Sea (2004), which is based at the University of Pittsburgh.

In conclusion, there is no better time to introduce a course on comparative family policy than today. It will provide a wonderful vehicle for understanding the culture and customs of our brothers and sisters throughout the world. Equally important, students may become so inspired that they begin to consider careers in international work, such as working with many of the (NGOs) that continue to emerge throughout the world. In short, I strongly suggest including such a course in the curricula if it does not already exist.

REFERENCES

Ahn, H. & Gilbert, N. (1992). Cultural diversity and sexual abuse prevention. *Social Service Review, 66,* 3, 410-427.

Australian Institute of Family Studies. (2004). Retrieved January 24, 2004, from www.aifs.gov.au.

Baker, M. (1995). *Canadian Family Policies: Cross-National Comparisons.* Toronto: Toronto University Press.

Clearinghouse on International Developments in Child, Youth and Family Policies (2004). Retrieved January 24, 2004, from http://www.childpolicyintl.org.

Clignet, R. (1991). Can American social science majors acquire an international perspective? *PS: Political Science & Politics, 24,* 68-72.

Council on International Educational Exchange. (2004). Retrieved January 24, 2004, from http://www.ciee.org.

Cox, R. (1993). Why is it difficult to teach comparative politics to American students? *PS: Political Science & Politic, 26* (1), 231-235.

Elazar, D. (1984). *American Federalism: A view from the states.* New York: Harper & Row.

Gauthier, A. H. (1996). *The state and the family: A comparative analysis of family policies in industrialized countries.* Oxford: Oxford University Press.

Ginsburg, N. (1992). *Divisions of welfare: A critical introduction to comparative social policy.* Thousand Oaks, CA: Sage.

Jansson, B. (2001). Why has the American welfare state been reluctant? In B. Jansson (Ed.), *The reluctant welfare state* (pp. 407-432). Belmont, CA: Wadsworth/Thomson Learning.

Kamerman, S. & Kahn, A. (1978). *Family policy: Government and families in fourteen countries.* New York: Columbia University Press.

Kaufman, F., Kuijsten, A., Schulze, H., & Strohmeier, K. (2002). *Family life and family policies in Europe: Problems and issues in comparative perspective.* Oxford: Oxford University Press.

Larson, L. (1980). *Comparative political analysis.* Chicago: Nelson-Hall Publishers.

Leeder, E. (2003). *The family in global perspective: A gendered journey.* Thousand Oaks, CA: Sage.

Morrison, T., Conaway, W., & Borden, G. (1994). *Kiss, bow, or shake hands: How to do business in sixty countries.* Holbrook, MA: Bob Adams.

Myrdal, A. & Myrdal, G. (1934). *The nation and the family: Crisis in the population question.* Stockholm: Albert Fonnier Forlag.

O'Hara, K. (1998). *Comparative family policy: Eight countries' stories.* Ottawa, ON: Renouf Publishing.

Pfenning, A. & Bahle, T. (2001). *Families and family policies in Europe: Comparative perspectives.* New York: Peter Lang Publishing.

Rainwater, L. & Smeeding, T. (2003). *Poor kids in a rich country: America's children in comparative perspective.* New York: Russell Sage Foundation.

Semester at Sea. (2004). Retrieved January 24, 2004, from http://www.semesterat sea.com/.

Smith, D., & Armstrong, S. (2002). *If the world were a village: A book about the world's people.* Tanawanda, NY: Kids Can Press.

United Nations Family Unit (2004). Retrieved January 24, 2004, from http://www.un.org/esa/socdev/family/familyunit.htm.

United Nations Wire (2004). Retrieved January 24, 2004, from http://www.unwire.org.

Vanier Institute of the Family (2004). Retrieved January 24, 2004, from http://www.vifamily.ca/.

Wisensale, S. (2001). The family and American politics. In S. Wisensale (Ed.), *Family leave policy: The political economy of work and family in America* (pp. 29-51). Armonk, NY: M.E. Sharpe.

Zimmerman, S. (1992). Political culture: Definitions and variations in 50 states. In S. Zimmerman (Ed.), *Family policies and family well-being: The role of political culture* (pp. 36-53). Thousand Oaks, CA: Sage.

Chapter 4

Breaking Down Cultural Barriers: An Evaluation of Cultural Competence Training for Family, Youth, and Community Science Educators

Lisa A. Guion
Lamont A. Flowers

The ongoing process of breaking down cultural barriers and becoming culturally competent begins with an honest assessment of our personal values and an examination of the worldviews that shape the way we view others. This is a difficult process for most people because, most likely, these culturally shaped "lenses" through which we view the world have been cultivated for years within our ethnic communities, neighborhoods, families, and/or tribes (Dresser, 1996). After self-assessment, the next step to becoming culturally competent is to learn how to respect cultural differences. In fact, showing appreciation for cultural diversity is the beginning of a rewarding journey toward building trust, cross-cultural communication, and competence in working with diverse audiences. Studying cultural traditions, norms, practices, values, and learning styles can also enable family, youth, and community science professionals to effectively deliver education/services to connect with culturally diverse individuals on a deeper level.

Despite intracultural similarities, all individuals, children, and families are unique. Therefore, the body of knowledge about a certain culture should be viewed as a guideline, not an absolute, serving to enhance services and communication rather than to stereotype individuals. General descriptions and guidelines will not apply to every person or situation, simply because there will always be exceptions

doi:10.1300/5609_04

when describing individuals. Also, several factors influence how closely an individual aligns with his or her culture. Such factors can include socioeconomic status, education, income level, and length of time in the United States (if foreign born), social associations/affiliations, etc. (Lynch & Hanson, 1997; Weaver, 2000).

Thus, the goal of cultural competence training is to gain insight into research-based information on cultural norms, values, beliefs, and practices. Cultural competence is an ongoing process that requires a thorough examination of the current research pertaining to cultural differences as well as meaningful and purposeful interactions with diverse individuals and families. In Cooperative Extension Service Programs, we have observed, in our interactions with family, youth, and community science professionals, that barriers between cultures are removed when there is understanding of others' differences, respect of others' points of view, progress toward cultural competence, and incorporation of cultural relevance into education/service delivery. The National Council on Family Relations (NCFR), recognizing the importance of culturally competent family practitioners and professionals, includes families in society as one of ten critical content areas for its Certification in Family Life Education program (NCFR, 2004a). The Ethnic Minority Section provides support and a forum for members of color, and keeps issues of diversity in the forefront of the organization's thinking and activity (NCFR, 2004b). Many other organizations are building support systems and resources to assist their personnel in meeting the challenge of providing education/services in a multicultural, pluralistic society.

BACKGROUND

The 2000 Census confirmed, what many speculated for years, that minority groups are rapidly increasing in the United States. To be sure, America is more ethnically, linguistically, and culturally diverse than ever before (Fix, Zimmermann, & Passel, 2001). This is due to four main factors:

1. large-scale immigration (legal and illegal),
2. globalization of goods, services, and finances,
3. current immigration policy that emphasizes family unification, and

4. the fact that the 2000 Census allowed people to mark more than one race for the first time in history (Riche, 2000).

The following U.S. Census Bureau (2000) statistics further reinforce this point:

1. Language is a very important part of one's culture. Nearly one in five Americans (17.9 percent of the population) over age five spoke a foreign language at home in 2000.
2. Foreign-born immigration is approaching levels that have not been realized since the years 1900-1910. The U.S. Immigration and Naturalization Service reports that 11 percent of the total U.S. population is foreign born. In the past two decades, 14.9 million foreign-born immigrants have been admitted to the United States.
3. People are recognizing their multiethnicity. In the 2000 Census, nearly 7 million people (2.4 percent of the entire population) identified with more than one race. This is significant given that this was the first time in the history of census taking that individuals were afforded the opportunity to share their complete ethnic composition. Projections are that this number may double during the next census (Fix, Zimmermann, & Passel, 2001).
4. Immigrants are settling throughout the country. For decades, six states (California, New York, Florida, Texas, Illinois, and New Jersey) have traditionally held the highest rates of immigration by far. However, in 2000, immigrant settlement into other states was double the pace of that found in the six traditional immigrant states (Fix, Zimmermann, & Passel, 2001).
5. Ethnic groups are moving into the suburbs. The 2000 Census revealed that in the past decade, the suburbs have become more ethnically diverse. Nonwhites residing in the suburbs increased from 19 percent (1990) to 27 percent (2000) across all suburban areas (Fix, Zimmermann, & Passel, 2001).
6. Over the next fifteen to twenty years in the United States, it is predicted that Latin Americans will account for 47 percent of the population growth, African Americans will account for 22 percent of the population growth, and Asian Americans and Native Americans combined will account for 18 percent of the population growth (Ting-Toomey, 1999).

Given these statistics and demographic data, it is only logical that family, youth, and community science programs need to invest more time and energy into teaching students and current practitioners to be more culturally competent. Students and practitioners need to learn about the cultures of those diverse individuals whom they currently serve or would like to serve. This knowledge will aid in developing relevant programs that reflect the unique interests and culture of their audiences.

CULTURAL COMPETENCE

Culture encompasses the values, beliefs, practices, norms, and languages of a group that have been learned, shared, and transmitted intergenerationally; it influences a person's feelings, thinking, and behavior (Hogan-Garcia, 2003; Pedersen, 2000). Cultural competence addresses three areas:

1. cultural awareness, understanding, and connecting with one's own ethnic identity and culture;
2. knowledge acquisition about other cultures; and
3. skill development for interacting, educating, and working with culturally diverse audiences (Fong & Furuto, 2001; Lynch & Hanson, 1997; Weaver, 2000; Lum, 1999).

The identification of personal norms, beliefs, and values is a prerequisite for understanding and respecting the importance of these constructs to others. Understanding shared cultural values of different ethnic groups in America requires learning information about the group, exposure to members of the group, and an awareness of the social, historical, and political dynamics of the group's existence in the United States.

The cornerstone of cultural competence is a better understanding of individuals within cultural groups that we currently serve and/or desire to serve. Knowledge of the history, culture, traditions, customs, language or dialect, religious or spiritual beliefs, art, music, and communication delivery and retrieval patterns is vital to educators in laying the foundation for true connections (Dresser, 1996; McPhatter, 1997). This knowledge helps educators better understand members of a particular community and how they interpret their world (Okun,

Fried, & Okun, 1999). Respecting and learning about culture promotes a focus on the positive characteristics and strengths of a community and the individuals that reside within it (Okun, Fried, & Okun, 1999). This leads to an appreciation of cultural differences. Corey and Corey (2003) assert that educators/helpers must first be aware of their own assumptions, biases, and values to become increasingly aware of the cultural values, biases, and assumptions of culturally different learners in nonjudgmental ways.

Cultural competence results from a deliberate, systematic, and long-term approach to change (Nash, 1999). Culturally competent educators recognize the constantly changing needs of the populations they serve. Change is the future; it cannot be avoided, and therefore should be viewed positively and embraced. Without change, there cannot be growth.

Culturally relevant family and consumer science programs are more effective and powerful because they are designed to address specific needs of a cultural community. Learning and respecting the particular needs of a cultural group in order to better serve people from that group is far more effective than simply doing what has always worked with other, more mainstream populations (McPhatter, 1997). Cultural competence also entails improving relationships with various ethnic communities and designing programs that are directly related to their needs, lives, and individual goals (Murphy & Nesby, 2002).

If programs are to effectively serve an increasingly diverse population, practitioners/educators must become more culturally aware, responsive, and competent. Culturally competent educators consider factors such as language, customs, ethnicity, family structure, and community/tribal dynamics when designing their programs (Lynch & Hanson, 1997). Once practitioners/educators have learned to fuse the strengths and perspectives of culturally diverse audiences into their programs, then services have the potential to flourish.

BUILDING CULTURAL COMPETENCE

One of the more obvious components of cultural competence is the importance of gaining a deeper understanding and respect for the differences between cultures. Finding commonalities and common ground is also important. However, misunderstanding, miscommunication, and conflict are based on differences, not commonalities (Weaver, 2000). Learning about cultural group norms and practices, contemplating community belief systems, and studying behavioral patterns all add layers to the overall package of cultural competence. Learn what is valued in a cultural community; values have a direct impact on behavior. Although it is inappropriate to stereotype ethnic groups with fixed, inflexible notions of how they will think or behave, education about general norms that have been observed by those who study cultural groups may help improve communication, program design, and delivery capabilities among family and consumer science professionals. Of course, some will not fit the cultural norms or will not subscribe to the same value system as others in their cultural community. However, a solid body of literature suggests that many individuals within a culture group do tend to hold some shared cultural values, norms, practices, and beliefs (Fong & Furuto, 2001; Lynch & Hanson, 1997; Ting-Toomey, 1999; Weaver, 2000). Knowledge of those shared cultural traits and characteristics is very useful in reducing culture shock and enhancing cross-cultural communication (Ting-Toomey, 1999; Weaver, 2000). When this knowledge is used flexibly and with good intentions to connect and communicate with individuals from a place of mutual respect, it can only assist in breaking down cultural barriers.

Strengthening Programs to Reach Diverse Audiences

A multistate, multiuniversity, and multidisciplinary team of Cooperative Extension specialists developed a curriculum, "Strengthening Programs to Reach Diverse Audiences," in response to a growing need to enhance the cultural competence of family, youth, and community science educators. This curriculum is comprised of six units containing a total of fourteen hands-on, interactive lessons. Each unit focuses on cultural awareness, knowledge, and skills needed by professionals as it relates to key aspects of planning and implementing culturally relevant programs for ethnically diverse children, youth, families, and communities.

Focus on Ethnic Diversity in the Curriculum

In this curriculum, the diverse audiences include the four major ethnic groups in the United States: African Americans, Asian Americans,

Hispanic/Latino Americans, and Native Americans. These groups are seen as primary due to their current population levels and projections for future growth when compared to other ethnic groups. Of course, differences will occur among individuals within an ethnic group based on many factors, such as one's level of ethnic identity, level of education, socioeconomic background, religion, and other factors (Okun, Fried, & Okun, 1999). However, a large body of literature documents some similar cultural attributes among members of specific ethnic groups, and this information cannot be overlooked (Fong & Furuto, 2001; Hogan-Garcia, 2003; Lynch & Hanson, 1997; Pedersen, 2000; Ting-Toomey, 1999; Weaver, 2000). This curriculum explores those cultural attributes in the context of planning and implementing programs. Finally, this curriculum focuses on increasing cultural competence in three domains: (a) cognitive, (b) affective, and (c) behavioral. Sue, Ivey, and Pedersen (1996) suggest that ethical and effective multicultural educators evolve from focused, concentrated, and ongoing training, resources, and support. This curriculum is an important first step in an ongoing process to meet the need for cultural competence training.

Theoretical Framework of Curriculum

The curriculum is grounded in the cooperative learning and constructivism theory of knowledge. Both theories position learners as active agents in the learning process, not passive receptacles into which knowledge is poured (Ahearn et. al, 2002). The role of the educator is that of a facilitator. Also, this curriculum is based on the experiential learning model (think, do, reflect). In keeping with these theoretical frameworks, interactive interest approaches and application exercises accompany each lesson. These hands-on activities promote learning through discussion, interaction, and reflection.

Scope and Organization of the Curriculum

Unit 1, the introductory unit, lays the foundation for the rest of the curriculum by expanding on participants' understanding of diversity. The unit provides a broad look at the impact of cultural diversity and the changing demographics of the United States, and offers recommendations for involving diverse audiences in family, youth, and community programming. Unit 2 discusses how cultural competence is a continuous process of assessing and broadening participants' knowledge of, and respect for, diverse individuals, which can significantly enhance the effectiveness of Extension professionals. Relying on literature from various fields, this unit also shares specific cultural norms, values, beliefs, practices, and learning styles of the four ethnic groups. Unit 3 provides strategies for enhancing marketing to diverse populations by utilizing three techniques: (1) personal marketing, (2) ethnic marketing, and (3) relationship marketing. Unit 4 discusses key strategies for uncovering and accessing the individual strengths/ skills, as well as organizational and institutional resources within a community to maximize and enhance Extension programs. These combined assets can be used to aid in program planning, program implementation, and volunteer development. Unit 5 provides strategies for learning ways to connect with diverse people when carrying out Extension instruction. This unit focuses on strategies and techniques for effectively instructing/teaching diverse individuals. Unit 6 presents strategies for dealing with issues such as burnout and stress. Exhibit 4.1 displays the outline of the curriculum, highlights the major lessons addressed in the curriculum, and lists the author(s) of each unit.

Curriculum Training

The curriculum was used in three eight-hour training sessions held as a preconference to a national Extension conference. The purpose of the training was to educate Extension professionals who work with children, youth, family, and community programs on the Strengthening Programs to Reach Diverse Audiences curriculum. More specifically, the curriculum training provided tools and educational resources to increase cultural awareness, knowledge, and skills related to planning programs for ethnically diverse audiences. Forty-five Extension family, youth, and community science professionals from twenty-eight different states across the nation participated in the training. Geographically, every region of the country was represented.

EXHIBIT 4.1. Strengthening Programs to Reach Diverse Audiences: Outline of Curriculum

UNIT 1

Understanding Diversity to Design Programs
(written by Lisa A. Guion and Cassandra Caldwell)

- Lesson 1—What is diversity and why is it important?
- Lesson 2—Programming considerations for ethnically diverse and at-risk audiences

UNIT 2

Planning Programs to Break Down Cultural Barriers
(written by Stephanie Sullivan Lytle and Lisa A. Guion)

- Lesson 1—Cultivating cultural competence
- Lesson 2—Connecting across cultures

UNIT 3

Marketing Programs to Diverse Audiences
(written by Samantha Chattaraj and Lisa A. Guion)

- Lesson 1—An introduction to personal marketing techniques
- Lesson 2—Strategies for marketing with diverse audiences
- Lesson 3—An introduction to relationship marketing

UNIT 4

Maximizing Assets of Diverse Communities to Enhance Programs
(written by Gae Broadwater and Lisa A. Guion)

- Lesson 1—Welcome to the neighborhood: A new way of looking at diverse communities
- Lesson 2—Strategies for conducting assets assessments in diverse communities
- Lesson 3—Building on the assets of diverse communities

UNIT 5

Effective Instruction for Diverse Audiences
(written by H. Wallace Goddard)

- Lesson 1—Connecting smart: Building bridges to the people you serve
- Lesson 2—Teaching smart: Designing your instruction to be effective with diverse audiences

(continued)

(continued)

UNIT 6

Working with Diverse Audiences Over Time
(written by Lisa A. Guion and Cassandra Caldwell)

* Lesson 1—Avoiding burnout when working with multineed audiences
* Lesson 2—Key issues of working with culturally and racially diverse audiences

TRAINING EVALUATION METHODOLOGY

Participants

Forty-five Extension professionals participated in the development programs, which utilized the curriculum: nine males and thirty-six females. The racial composition of the Extension professionals was as follows: five African Americans, one Asian American/Pacific Islander, thirty-eight whites, and one Hispanic American. Twenty-six Extension professionals had a master's degree or higher, seventeen had a bachelor's degree, one had an associate's degree, and one attended business or trade school. Eighteen Extension professionals had twelve years or more experience, one had nine-eleven years of experience, four had six-eight years experience, thirteen had three-five years of experience, and eight had less than two years of experience. One person chose not to answer the question pertaining to his or her length of service as an Extension professional.

Preprogram Evaluation

Before the program began, participants completed a pre-program evaluation survey. The preprogram evaluation consisted of a fifteen-item survey designed to measure participants' demographic characteristics, openness to diversity attitudes, and diversity training needs. The preprogram evaluation contained a quantitative component as well as a qualitative component. The quantitative component contained a six-item demographic questionnaire (e.g., gender, educational attainment, years of service, etc.) and an openness to diversity measure consisting of an eight-item, Likert-type scale (1 = strongly disagree to 5 = strongly agree). The scale contained items that sought to measure the extent to which participants maximized opportunities to learn about diverse ideas and individuals (e.g., I enjoy having discussions with people whose ideas and values are different from my own; Learning about people from different cultures is a very important part of my professional development). Higher scores on the scale indicated greater openness and tolerance for diversity. The openness to diversity scale was modified from an earlier study conducted by Flowers and Pascarella (1999). The scale was chosen because the internal consistency data were appropriate and suggested that the scale contained homogenous items that accurately measured the intended concepts of interest. Using data from the preprogram evaluation, the coefficient alpha for this scale was .75. The remainder of the preprogram evaluation contained one open-ended item designed to determine participants' preprogram diversity training needs (i.e., Identify the knowledge, values, and/or skills that you would like to obtain as a result of participating in this program that will help you to work with diverse ethnic groups and/or multineed audiences).

Postprogram Evaluation

Following the completion of the program, participants completed a twelve-item, postprogram evaluation survey designed to measure participants' perceptions of the extent to which the curriculum provided participants with the knowledge, values, and/or skills to work with diverse ethnic groups. The postprogram evaluation also contained a quantitative component and a qualitative component. The quantitative component contained the aforementioned, eight-item, openness to diversity scale. Using data from the postprogram evaluation, the coefficient alpha for this scale was .82. The remainder of the post-program evaluation contained four open-ended items designed to determine participants' postprogram knowledge gain and skill development, as well as the extent to which the information covered in the curriculum could assist them in planning more effective programs for diverse audiences. The following open-ended items were used in this evaluation:

1. To what extent do you believe this program has provided you with the knowledge, values, and/or skills to work with diverse ethnic groups?

2. If someone asked you what was the most important idea or information that you learned as a result of participating in this program, what would you tell him or her?
3. How can something you learned from this program help you in either planning or carrying out your programs with diverse ethnic groups and/or multineed audiences?
4. Is there anything related to your perceptions or views of the program I haven't asked that you want to add?

Data Analysis Procedures

Data analysis for the program evaluation occurred in a two-stage process. First, mean difference was calculated to measure the magnitude of the change in openness to diversity. Standard deviations for the prepro- gram evaluation, postprogram evaluation, and mean difference were also computed. A dependent samples t-test procedure was then utilized to determine if the mean difference in participants' preprogram evaluation and postprogram evaluation scores was statistically significant. The dependent samples t-test procedure was deemed appropriate in program evaluation because of the ability of the procedure to determine if significant differences existed between the same group of examinees who took a pretest and a posttest (Cloughesy, Zahler, and Rellergert 2001). Also, we computed an effect size estimate by subtracting participants' pre- and postprogram evaluation scores on the openness to diversity scale and dividing the mean difference by the pooled standard deviation (Rosnow & Rosenthal, 1996). This effect-size estimate measured (in standard deviation units) the practical significance of the mean difference. In the second stage of data analysis, the qualitative data were analyzed for content (Neuendorf, 2002). Participant responses to the open-ended questions were grouped by question categories for coding purposes. Common themes were sought for each category.

RESULTS

Table 4.1 displays the means, standard deviations, mean difference, and effect size. The mean difference was statistically significant. The effect size result was moderate in value indicating that the practical significance of the mean difference was meaningful. The effect size result also suggests that the curriculum may serve as an

TABLE 4.1. Means, standard deviations, mean difference, and effect size for the pretest and posttest.

	Mean	Pretest standard deviation	Mean	Posttest standard deviation	Mean differ- ence	Standard deviation of gain score	Effect size
Openness to Diversity Scale	34.44	3.52	36.58	3.28	2.14*	2.16	.63

*$p < .01$

effective intervention in terms of improving Extension professionals' willingness to be open to diverse ideas and cultures.

Based on Guion and Flowers (2001), qualitative data assessing participants' reactions concerning the effectiveness and quality of the curriculum were also obtained. As shown in Exhibit 4.2, the participants overwhelmingly supported the curriculum. One participant commented that the curriculum "fostered more appreciation for the strength of diversity." Another participant noted that the curriculum "has given facts to help build a case for reaching new audiences." It was evident from these and other responses that the curriculum met all of its goals and objectives. However, some suggestions for improvements were listed by participants such as increasing the duration of the training and conducting follow-up training after participants have had an opportunity to try some of the strategies outlined in the curriculum. A few requested that Extension professionals from their local county level who are successfully working with diverse audiences also be present at the training. Another recommendation was to include other groups in the curriculum beyond the four ethnic groups that were targeted. For example, a few participants shared that their communities are experiencing influxes from other ethnic groups (e.g., Eastern Europeans, Africans).

CONCLUSION

Family, youth, and community science professionals will continually need to acquire additional skills that will enable them to work with

EXHIBIT 4.2. Selected Reponses from the Posttest Program Evaluation Questionnaire

Question 1

To what extent do you believe this program has provided you with the knowledge, values, and/or skills to work with diverse ethnic groups and/or multineed audiences?

- This workshop was wonderfully put together. I can't wait to use it and train others on it.
- It appeals to all learning styles and provides the written reference to return to.
- I am leaving here today with tools and knowledge and will work toward the development of skills that will allow me to reach audiences I have not reached in the past and I will be able to help county faculty in their efforts to reach our state's diverse populations.
- I am looking forward to utilizing these excellent resources. I find them very helpful.
- Excellent—wonderful compilation of resources, easy to use lessons, and framework. This is one of the best, if not the best, workshops and curriculum on diversity that I've ever had.

Question 2

If someone asked you what was the most important idea or information that you learned as a result of participating in this program, what would you tell him or her?

- I loved all the activities provided in this workshop. It was a good mix of hands-on activities and lecture.
- People don't "fit" general categories.
- That we can intelligently talk about diversity and issues which may come from facing new ideas.
- Really thinking about diversity before planning, and acting, as well as developing relationships.
- To be open to new ideas and to listen to others.

Question 3

How can something you learned from this program help you in either planning or carrying out your programs with diverse ethnic groups and/or multineed audiences?

- I work with many diverse audiences so this will help me in understanding the groups that I work with more. I will also be able to provide more meaningful resources.
- It arrives just as I am preparing to market a new program.

(continued)

- It has given me a model to begin looking at other audiences not included in this program.
- This information challenges me to consider that ethnic values also impact education.
- I have not had the opportunity or training or knowledge to work with Native Americans, and this is a great vehicle of introduction.

persons from various cultural and ethnic backgrounds (Ingram, 1999; Schauber & Castania, 2001). This contention was also supported, by Williams (1992, p. 5) who asserted: "If Extension is to truly address the needs of both traditional and diverse audiences, this commitment must be communicated at all levels and made a part of each job description and plan of work—regardless of the discipline, initiative, or program area." In addition, all Extension professionals must figure out ways to use the diversity that exists in their offices as well as in their communities to promote the development and advancement of all children, youths, and families (Schauber & Castania, 2001). In order to provide current and relevant training opportunities for Extension professionals, additional resources will need to be developed that respond to evolving issues that impact various communities all over the country.

This chapter provided details on the design, implementation, and program evaluation results for a diversity curriculum. This curriculum, while designed for Extension, can be used by any family and consumer science-related organization/institution to assist their practitioners and/or students with: (1) understanding diversity, (2) planning culturally relevant programs, and (3) evaluating the goals of diversity-based programs and services. The results of this program evaluation support the continued use and evaluation of this curriculum. Specifically, the participants who took part in this evaluation reported significantly higher scores on a measure of openness to diver- stiy. In addition, several program participants noted that the curriculum was informative and useful in helping them to increase their ability to work with ethnically diverse audiences.

The primary limitation of this research was the small sample size used in the program evaluation. Thus, it is not possible to generalize these findings to all Extension professionals. Given the innovative design of this curriculum as well as the exploratory evidence from this program evaluation, it is clear that this curriculum may be used to enhance cultural competency levels for Extension professionals. However, additional research is needed to confirm these results for a nationally representative and large sample of Extension professionals. Future research is needed involving multivariate research designs to statistically control for variables that may have also confounded the results of this study (e.g., gender and age). Last, it was clear from the preprogram evaluation data that our sample included participants who scored reasonably high on the openness to diversity scale. The standard deviation for the pre- and postprogram evaluation further indicated that the participants did not vary much with respect to their openness to diversity. This lack of variability in the group compounded with the fact that participants scored very high on the openness to diversity scale in the pre- and postprogram evaluation, indicates that this group may have been predisposed to the types of ideas and issues discussed in the curriculum. Future studies that include participants who differ markedly on the preprogram evaluation may yield better evidence regarding the effectiveness of this curriculum to improve cultural competence. Despite these limitations, this study, which represents an initial attempt to collect and analyze data on the effects of this curriculum on Extension professionals, suggests that this curriculum is worthwhile and may result in significant gains in multicultural knowledge, values, and skills.

REFERENCES

Ahearn, A., Childs-Bowen, D., Coady, M., Dickson, K, Heintz, C., Hughes, K., et al. (2002). *The diversity kit: An introductory resource for social change in education.* Providence, RI: Brown University.

Cloughesy, M., Zahler, D., & Rellergert, M. (2001). Using pre- and post- tests to evaluate the achievement of short course learning objectives. *Journal of Extension, 39*(2). Retrieved June 17, 2003, from http://joe.org/joe/2001april/tt4.html.

Corey, M. S. & Corey, G. (2003). *Becoming a helper.* Pacific Grove, CA: Brooks/Cole.

Dresser, N. (1996). *Multicultural manners: New rules of etiquette for a changing society.* New York: John Wiley & Sons.

Fix, M., Zimmermann, W., & Passel, J. S. (2001). *The integration of immigrant families in the United States.* Washington, DC: The Urban Institute.

Flowers, L. A. & Pascarella, E. T. (1999). Does college racial composition influence the openness to diversity of African American students? *Journal of College Student Development, 40,* 405-417.

Fong, R. & Furuto, S. M. (Eds.) (2001). *Culturally competent practice: Skills, interventions, and evaluations.* Needham Heights, MA: Allyn and Bacon.

Guion, L. A. & Flowers, L. A. (2001). *Using qualitative research in planning and evaluating extension programs.* Retrieved May 21, 2002, from the University of Florida, Institute for Food and Agricultural Sciences Web site: http://edis.ifas.ufl.edu/pdffiles/FY/FY39200.pdf.

Hogan-Garcia, M. (2003). *The four skills of cultural diversity competence: A process for understanding and practice.* Pacific Grove, CA: Brooks/Cole.

Ingram, P. D. (1999). Attitudes of extension professionals toward diversity education in 4-H programs. *Journal of Extension, 37*(1). Retrieved June 17, 2003, from http://joe.org/joe/1999february/a3.html.

Lum, D. (1999). *Culturally competent practice: A framework for growth and action.* Pacific Grove, CA: Brooks/Cole.

Lynch, E. W. & Hanson, M. S. (1997). *Developing cross-cultural competence: A guide for working with children and their families* (Second edition). Baltimore, MD: Paul H. Brookes.

McPhatter, A. R. (1997). Cultural competence in child welfare: What is it? How do we achieve it? What happens without it? *Child Welfare, 76,* 255-278.

Murphy, E. & Nesby, T. (2002). *A map for inclusion: Building cultural competency.* Pullman, WA: Cooperative Extension Washington State University.

Nash, K. A. (1999). *Cultural competence: A guide for human service agencies.* Washington, DC: Child Welfare League of America Press.

National Council on Family Relations (NCFR). (2004a). Certified Family Life Educator Program. Retrieved March 2, 2004, from http://www.ncfr.org/cfle/c_certification.htm.

National Council on Family Relations (NCFR). (2004b). Ethnic Minority Section. Retrieved March 3, 2004, from http://www.asn.csus.edu/em-ncfr/.

Neuendorf, K. A. (2002). *The content analysis guidebook.* Thousand Oaks, CA: Sage.

Okun, B. F., Fried, J., & Okun, M. L. (1999). *Understanding diversity: A learning-as-practice primer.* Pacific Grove, CA: Brooks/Cole.

Pedersen, P. (2000). *A handbook for developing multicultural awareness* (Third edition) Alexandria, VA: American Counseling Association.

Riche, M. F. (2000). *America's diversity and growth: Signposts for the 21st century.* Washington, DC: Population Reference Bureau.

Rosnow, R. L. & Rosenthal, R. (1996). Computing contrasts, effect sizes, and counternulls on other people's published data: General procedures for research consumers. *Psychological Methods, 1,* 331-340.

Schauber, A. C. & Castania, K. (2001). Facing issues of diversity: Rebirthing the Extension service. *Journal of Extension, 39*(6). Retrieved June 17, 2003, from http://joe.org/joe/2001december/comm2.html.

Sue, D. W., Ivey, A. E., & Pedersen, P. (1996). *A theory of multicultural counseling and therapy.* Pacific Grove, CA: Brooks/Cole.

Ting-Toomey, S. (1999). *Communicating across cultures.* New York: The Guilford Press.

U.S. Census Bureau (2000). Mapping census 2000: The geography of U.S. diversity. Retrieved February 15, 2003, from http://www.census.gov/population/www/cen2000/atlas.html.

Weaver, G. R. (2000). *Culture, communication and conflict: Readings in intercultural relations* (Second edition). Boston: Pearson.

Williams, L. (1992). Diversity involves us all. *Journal of Extension, 30*(3). Retrieved June 17, 2003, from http://www.joe.org/joe/1992fall/tp2.html.

Chapter 5

The Cultural Transformation Model: Promoting Cultural Competence Through International Study Experiences

Sylvia M. Asay
Maha N. Younes
Tami James Moore

The September 11, 2001, terrorist attacks on American soil stunned the world. Educators were compelled to discuss international issues as they assisted their students to make sense of the national tragedy. Americans found themselves being educated by the media about distant cultures, fundamentals of different religions, and world geography. The veil of ignorance had been forcefully lifted and the time had come for American postsecondary education to prepare students in family science programs for the challenges of a new world order which demands the integration of political, economic, social, and cultural competencies. The emerging global community transcends boundaries compelling nations to clarify cultural ideals and values that are crucial for the enhancement of international relationships.

Healy (2001) stressed that countries across the globe redesign their own social policies to be more compatible with other nations around the world. She posits that global interdependence is "an irrefutable fact" which countries must embrace in order to overcome their tendency toward isolationism (p. 123). Education must undergo some revolutionary changes to respond effectively to the challenges of the new world. Diaz (1992, p. 19) advocated, "American education must make significant adjustments to meet the challenge of the demographic

doi:10.1300/5609_05

changes of the twenty-first century." Banks (1992) supported Diaz's assertion and emphasized that multicultural education is imperative to ensure that the "nation's citizens acquire the knowledge, attitudes, and skills needed to survive" in the next century. He further adds that in the "twenty-first century, a nation whose citizens cannot negotiate on the world's multicultural global stage will be tremendously disadvantaged, and its very survival will be imperiled" (p. 35).

Preparing students for futures as professionals in a global environment requires facilitating their growth in a distinct realm—cultural competence. Cross, Bazron, Dennis, and Isaacs (1989) define cultural competence as sensitivity, knowledge, and skills relating to the unique needs of culturally diverse populations. Orlandi (1992) defined cultural competence as "a set of academic and interpersonal skills that allow individuals to increase their understanding and appreciation of cultural differences and similarities, within, among, and between groups" (pp. 3-4). This definition is especially applicable as it relates to the implicit mission of most international study tours and experiences offered by higher education institutions. Participation in such tours propels students into a process of cultural transformation leading to the development of cultural competence. Lum (2003) asserts that cultural competence emerges along a "continuum of social skill and personality development" (p. 7). International study experiences provide the intensity, depth, and breadth to help students along that continuum.

Empowering adult learners to incorporate new insights about the diversity of our world demands the development of innovative pedagogies that become part of the environment learners are studying. Daloz (1986, p. 152) stresses the importance of helping learners "to develop a new vision of themselves based on their own experiences rather than images they have absorbed from others." This is especially critical in helping adult learners overcome societal stereotypes already embedded into their belief system about different cultures. Merely infusing multicultural issues into the curriculum is no longer sufficient in the preparation of future practitioners. Purposeful action must be taken to transform curriculum; such a process "wrenches internalized values, and contests assumptions held so deeply that to challenge them feels as if one is fighting nature" (Friedman 1996, p. 2). Simply educating students about other cultures in a classroom setting lacks the contextual richness that can be acquired through direct interaction such as personal observations and communication.

In the traditional classroom, biases may be confronted superficially, cultural insecurities can go unrecognized, and limited change is made in the students' beliefs and behaviors. Participation in an international study experience provides the opportunity to immerse the student wholly into a different culture, experiencing the language, worldview, and food differences that define a culture and manifest its expression to those outside its boundaries.

RESEARCH STRATEGY

International Study Tours

It was the original intent of the researchers to understand the experiences of participants engaged in international study tours and the impact that such tours have on their educational experience. After securing necessary Institutional Review Board research approval, fifty-four college students and adult learners from three separate groups were asked to describe their experiences through semistructured questionnaires before, during, and after their summer session study tour. Although no interviews were conducted for the purpose of data gathering, extensive information was gained through voluntary questionnaires. The pretour questionnaire focused on demographics and expectations of the study tour, while the midpoint and posttour questionnaires focused on the students' experiences. All participants were traveling to European countries from the same Midwest University during approximately the same period of time. The first tour traveled to four Scandinavian countries. The focus of the tour was to examine social policies and it was highly structured with lectures, agency tours, and nightly discussions. The second tour traveled throughout Italy. The focus of this tour was to examine art and its history. This tour was semistructured and included some instruction. The third tour traveled to England, France, and Italy. Although this tour was not highly structured, it included several directed experiences for students who were studying interior design and family studies. To achieve accountability, the researchers were also tour group leaders who shared the same experiences as the participants.

As the rich data were analyzed from all three tours, a set of themes emerged that seemed to point to a surprisingly common theoretical rendition of reality. Although their tour destinations, tour structures, and areas of interest were different, the experiences of the participants began to naturally fall into statements of relationships and common themes. According to Strauss and Corbin (1990), these commonalities represent the foundation for a study using grounded theory methodology. As a result, the research question was refocused to provide the researchers with additional flexibility to explore in depth the emerging phenomena as the data unfolded the rich details of the participants' experiences throughout the study tour. The purpose of the present study became an examination of the impact that international study tours have on changing students' perspectives about culture.

Although information was collected at three different points during the tour, the researchers initially used open coding to categorize the data into a common set of characteristics that described the participants' experiences using the process of memoing (Creswell, 1998). Following the tours, the authors combined the data to discover a central phenomenon known as axial coding (Creswell, 1998) leading to the creation of a conceptual model. The model was then cross-checked with the original data to look for evidence to support the central phenomenon until saturation occurred as the data began to repeat the same information. The researchers were careful to identify causal and intervening conditions as well as the context in which the statements were made in forming the new theory. The idea that this experience was not only short-term but an immersion into another culture was considered and the connections to cultural shock were advanced.

Although a conceptual model often represents a change and movement forward, the Cultural Transformation Model that developed as a result of this project was designed to demonstrate more than that. Such a model was needed to illustrate the changes in cultural perspective that participants experience while engaged on a study tour, as well as a recognition that this change process may be ongoing and should not be limited to one particular tour experience or space of time. An open and upward spiral seemed to describe the phenomenon most accurately (See Figure 5.1). The following phases of the model describe the changes that the students in this study made in their understanding of culture while on the study tour experience. Each phase of the Cultural Transformation Model outlined utilizes the language that participants used in describing their journey. What emerges is a mosaic that is assembled through the students' unique experiences.

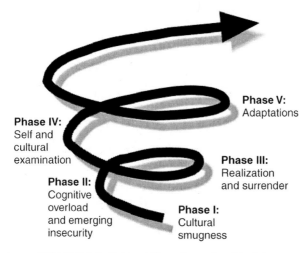

FIGURE 5.1. Cultural Transformation Model.

THE CULTURAL TRANSFORMATION MODEL: PHASES I-V

Phase I: Cultural Smugness

It seems necessary to begin phase I by including the profile of participants in order for the readers to identify their cultural background. Of the fifty-four students who participated in the three international study tours, fifty-two considered themselves Caucasian, one Hispanic, and one Asian. Twenty-six of the participants had previous international travel experience, and only half of the twenty-six had traveled as part of an organized international study group. All participants grew up in the Midwest and attended a university setting that was mostly homogenous and representative of the dominant Euro-American culture. Students' experiences in the early part of the international experience reveal a sense of cultural smugness and utilization of the "American way" as a comparative tool against which the value of all other cultures is assessed.

American society provides "whites" with a sense of entitlement that minority out-groups are deprived of (Helms, 1995). This entitlement translates into privileges that members of the dominant culture take for granted and come to expect in their interactions with others.

Students are no different. In the early phases of the international experience, their sense of smugness is quickly challenged as they realize that their rules of entitlement no longer apply to them as foreigners in other countries.

National and cultural pride was strongly expressed during this phase as students commented repeatedly: "I'm glad I am an American," "I'm thankful to be living in America," and "People want to live just like Americans." Students also frequently expressed comments related to what they perceived as the Americanization of European countries: "I can't believe how Americanized they are." Interestingly enough, many students expressed American ownership of the English language as a few asserted that "everyone caters to us and *our* language" and "they speak *our* language." These ethnocentric comments seem to mask the ignorance that most students have regarding the origin of their own ancestry and history. Either way, these remarks support the need for stronger educational emphasis on history and culture.

Smugness also translates into prejudice and judgmentalism that hinders positive interactions with members of a different culture. Students expressed feeling inconvenienced by the different cultural standards imposed on foreigners and resented having to "live with the lower standards," the difficulties of "having to deal with other cultures," and more troubling, judging people in other cultures as "rude" and lacking courtesy for not using the same social graces stressed in American society. Students touring the Scandinavian region were shocked by the absence of daily exchanges they are accustomed to, such as "Excuse me," "Sorry," "Please," and "Thank you." A student from another tour expressed her concern clearly by pointing out "how rude the French are to Americans." Students on the tour to Italy, France, and England commented on the "dirty places." Others said, "I had the expectation that it would be clean like the U.S.," "Everything is too small for me," and "Too many people in one country."

Phase II: Cognitive Overload and Emerging Insecurity

The cultural immersion and emotional bombardment participants experience on these international study experiences eventually led to feelings of frustration and a growing sense of insecurity that seemed to evolve into an internal outrage. This characterizes Phase II in which students made comments such as "I am not as confident as I thought I was" and this experience "takes me out of my comfort zone." The intensifying sense of insecurity is aggravated by what they believe members of the host culture think of them. As one participant commented, "Some really like Americans and others think we are idiots."

Language barriers contribute to the increasing lack of confidence; "It is interesting how one feels as though others are talking about them when others speak a different language." Some said, "I like it more in countries where I can communicate," and reported feeling excited "when I finally hear someone speak English or eat something familiar." Still, language remained an inconvenience as many indicated they were "having a difficult time with the language" and understanding what was expected of them by the host culture.

This phase is also characterized by feelings of anger at being inconvenienced by personal safety issues such as "pickpockets, losing items, [being] afraid and unsafe, crazy driving." Other inconveniences listed were "rudeness of people," "would have liked electricity and daily conveniences," and "having a hard time eating the food." This phase is truly paradoxical in that participants purposefully sought the international experience to be challenged and to learn, yet they resist opening themselves to experiences outside their comfort zones and cling to the safety of the group and all that is familiar to them.

Phase III: Realization and Surrender

Being immersed in a foreign culture places majority-culture students in minority status, perhaps for the first time in their lives. The realization that they are like a small fish in a big pond emerges as they recognize the enormity and diversity of the world they live in. Emotionally exhausted by the intensity of Phase II, participants begin to reconcile their place in the world. Comments like: "There are many different cultures in this world, not just mine," "There really is a whole other world out there," and "There are other cultures other than ours and they all have worth" were expressed frequently during this phase. Although recognizing the worth of other cultures promotes students' appreciation of the history and norms of those cultures, it is bitter-sweet as it leads to self-doubt and a more critical view of themselves and their culture. Participants verified this change by noting the cultural depth demonstrated by members of other cultures: "They are so in-tuned to their heritage," "They have culture and we have very little," and "It is an eye opener to see how arrogant and ignorant Americans are to think that everyone should just talk English."

Participants at this stage reach the lowest point in their "self talk" as they struggle with letting go of what is safe and familiar to them. With much ambivalence, they surrender their old way of thinking and begin to embrace a new way of viewing the world. Some begin to feel betrayed by the sheltered life that has allowed them to see the world from a restricted perspective. One student said, "Things that I always thought were common knowledge are not always thought of in other cultures." One commented, "This trip has opened my eyes to new things. The world seems just a little bit smaller now."

Phase IV: Self and Cultural Examination

Learning about the world becomes a personal discovery process as participants prepare themselves to become one with the world. This entails the shedding of one's ignorance, opening one's self to new knowledge, and welcoming what may be uncomfortable. A candid and mostly unconscious inventory of personal and cultural deficits is carried out as some stereotypes and beliefs may be dispensed of while others are modified. Numerous students made observations such as "I don't like the unknown," "I have learned that I have a tough time adjusting, I don't like change very much," "I have learned about my strengths as well as weaknesses," and "I don't know as much as I thought I did."

This challenging inventory leads participants to a stronger understanding of the need to be flexible in their worldview. They begin to recognize the vitality of being open-minded in order to reap the personal and educational benefits of the international experience. Many note the importance of "staying open-minded, maintaining objectivity" and confess "I have learned that I may not be as open-minded as I thought." Comments such as "I have learned how much there is to learn about life and people in general," "We as Americans do take many things for granted and are much more judgmental," and "I learned I shouldn't be so ignorant and self absorbed in my own world. I need to be more open to change" were common.

The personal reflective process evolves into thinking critically of the American culture as students write "I notice how spoiled I really am," "We are very spoiled with what we have in our living," "I think I am a very spoiled American," and "Now I know how people feel when they come to the U.S." It is essential to note the role of language in getting students to feel like outsiders and to make a comparative observation to what others visiting the United States may feel. Participants' preoccupation with language becomes an issue that they tackle throughout the international experience. They express countless concerns: "They speak our language plus others. It makes me jealous," "Not everyone has a positive attitude towards others who speak English. I find myself ashamed of the fact that I only speak English and I can't speak any other language," and "I expect them to speak my language when I haven't tried to learn another."

Efforts made to blend with the host culture seemed futile when language issues appeared beyond negotiation. The appearance of blending in became more important as one participant indicated, "I think that with my skin and light hair, I don't feel out of place until I talk."

This self-examination phase is painful but not without rewards as it leads students to a less judgmental stance, increased openness, and heightened sensitivity to people who may be deemed outsiders in the United States. This newly found personal and cultural humility paves the way for a healthier mode of interaction within the global community and a more enlightened citizenship in their own country.

Phase V: Adaptations

Having experienced the unsavory reality identified in the self-examination phase, participants are in a more suitable position to embrace the personal changes needed for them to become more competent players in the global community. Self-examination becomes an avenue leading to growth, as evident in the following comments: "I need to realize that there are so many different people in the world and that taking time to understand them will help me to grow as a person," "We need to be more tolerant of others, especially when we are in their country," and "I now have more respect for people of different cultures."

Students begin to foster, in themselves and others, qualities such as humility, cultural sensitivity, and openness in order to promote personal and cultural change. This change begins with the recognition that while proficiency in many languages may be impossible, making a commitment to learn at least one language other than English is achievable. Several expressed comments such as "I would like to learn to speak another language." One participant shared, "I am learning that there is no 'right way' or 'one way' of doing things," while another pointed out that learning takes place anywhere and anytime by "learning about people and learning from people."

As an outcome of this transformation process, some students may take on additional responsibility and personal accountability. They begin to perceive themselves as representative of their own culture and worry about "giving people in other countries the wrong impression." What began as cultural supremacy is replaced with cultural responsibility and a new way to define one's self and culture in relation to others in the world.

DISCUSSION

The data gathered in this study suggest that a developmental process encompasses the students' perspectives during international study experiences. Several existing theories explain pieces of this process, but none fully explores the transformational change of attitudes and behaviors of these students, the lasting impact, or the necessary contexts for such change to occur.

A review of the existing literature discloses two existing theories that partially explain the findings in this study: cultural shock and transformational learning. Winkelman (1994) builds upon the concept of *cultural shock*. He suggests that such shock is normal in foreign culture environments, although those experiencing it may not recognize it or respond effectively to its existence. He believes that such shock is caused in part by cognitive overload and behavioral inadequacies. Because intercultural effectiveness is based on understanding and adaptation of behaviors, cultural shock would appear to be best resolved with a social learning approach to preparing students for such an experience. He believes that cultural shock can be minimized by preparing students for problems (e.g., preparation meetings) before the experience and by identifying resources that will promote coping and adjustment.

Although minimizing student discomfort was something that leaders desired and perceived as a justifiable goal, one wonders whether such cushioning is beneficial to the learning of the student. Is being uncomfortable more conducive to sustained attitude and behavioral change? Bochner (1986) rejects the *adjustment model* suggested by cultural shock theorists, preferring *a culture learning* model. He posits that culture learning avoids implications of relative culture superiority inherent in the concept of adjustment. The model that evolved in this study challenges Bochner's ideas. Expectations of cultural superiority among students seemed common. Phase I, Cultural Smugness, is expressed by students in phrases rich with preconceived feelings of superiority.

When the goal of learning is to bring about change in a sustainable way, balancing the student's experience may be a better goal. Moore (1995) found that travel experience was positively related to the development of multicultural awareness of educators in regard to both their personal and professional behaviors. In that same study, mandated classroom instruction on multicultural concepts had no significant impact on those levels. Travel experience supported sustained and systemic change in participants' attitudes and behaviors. Therefore, permitting participants to ponder their own sense of discomfort yields a therapeutic value that should not be overlooked. Washington (1981) also found classroom learning to be ineffective in long-term student change. Her study of a five-day antiracism/multicultural education training workshop showed negligible, even declining, attitudinal and behavioral changes among the participants. Bennett (1988) reported that required multicultural education courses had an immediate impact on the attitudes and knowledge of preservice teachers; however, gains were reportedly lost within the year.

Why is cultural immersion more effective in transforming students' perspectives? Attitudes and behaviors are not easily changed. They are products of long-term creation and perpetual support. Merzirow (1991) and Daloz (1986) have written extensively on transformative learning. Merzirow (1991) defines *transformative learning* as the process of making meaning from our experiences through reflection, critical reflection, and critical self-reflection—all uncomfortable experiences. Key concepts, as discussed by Merzirow, include a disorienting dilemma and self-examination with feelings of guilt or shame. Discomfort seems to compel participants to change and motivates them to seek experiences that validate their new perspectives. In addition, Daloz (1986) redefines the reflection elements and emphasizes the personal change within the transformative learning process. Both approaches support elements of this new model, particularly the overload and insecurity of Phase II and the adjustments made in the following phases to alleviate the negative affective elements of the experience.

The Cultural Transformation Model emerging from the data presented in this study seems to support the idea that attitudes are systemically changed only when participants experience discomfort and are bound to find a new balance, or comfort. Piaget, as sited in Oakes and Lipton (1999), used the concepts of disequilibrium and equilibrium to explain the energy, tension, sense of balance and imbalance, and even the motivation that drives the whole cognitive process. Oakes and Lipton suggest the importance of helping students identify the tension of "not knowing" as curiosity or a "drive" or a need to know. Helping students reframe their discomfort and anxiety normalizes their experiences and supports their emerging cultural transformation.

Bodger (1998) found that when compared to the traditional classroom setting, an international study tour provides a personal experience of an event, place, or issue that cannot be duplicated through other pedagogies. Recognizing that the international study experience is superior to classroom presentations of cultural concepts, it becomes important in the design and delivery of such tours to retain a certain level of discomfort for the learner. The model that emerges from this grounded theory study includes these components (cognitive overload, emerging insecurity, and role reversal) while also providing a safe, guided opportunity for self-examination and reflection. The international cultural experience changes the participants in deep and meaningful ways.

CONCLUSION

There is little doubt as to the benefits of international study experiences on transforming the cultural perspectives of participants. Such immersions are filled with a barrage of multifaceted cultural challenges, emotionally exhilarating yet unsettling personal realizations, and intellectual discoveries that are difficult to attain any other way. Educators and tour leaders must determine the degree of discomfort that students need to experience during the international study experiences. The intent should not be the pursuit of unsettling and even painful personal and educational realizations. Rather, leaders should allow the unfolding of a naturally occurring culturally transformative process.

Two important issues that need to be considered when preparing students for cultural immersion experiences are *who* is traveling and *where* they will be traveling. Leaders need to take into account the student's cultural background, travel experience, socioeconomic status, and disciplinary or academic orientation. The destination is a determining factor in the degree of pretour preparation required; the more diverse the host culture from the students' own background, the more traumatic the experience is likely to be. The degree of difficulty associated with food, language, customs, values, and other societal norms will determine the degree of discomfort students may experience.

Some limitations exist in the current study. Though shock and discomfort were present to a significant degree, the fact that participants on the three international study experiences were mostly Caucasians touring European cultures that shared similar physical characteristics and cultural ideology, may have cushioned their psyche from more extreme culture shock. Touring Asia or Africa where physical and cultural differences are more noticeable will yield more intense discomfort as participants would also have to negotiate communication and food issues more directly. Participants also had varied travel experience; some never traveled outside of their own state while others had some international travel experience. As travelers become more experienced, they become more skilled at negotiating cultural differences and more open to accepting diversity. Interestingly enough, the same issues that limit this study also strengthen it. This is evident in the similar themes and experiences that emerged despite the different focus, structure, and leadership style of each group. Groups were not informed of the participation of other groups in the study.

Recognizing that cultural immersion through international study tours is a useful method for developing cultural competencies in learners, the model that emerges from this study is worthy of further exploration. Future research is needed to evaluate whether the attitudinal and behavioral changes are sustainable in the longterm. It would be interesting to know how the international study experience impacts the perceptions and feelings or thoughts that participants experience in response to current world tensions and the clash of world ideologies. Replicating this study with a group of culturally diverse students may yield insights leading to modification of the Cultural Transformation Model. It would also be fascinating to conduct the same study with tours traveling to Asia and Africa.

Although not all the participants of this study were family science students, the outcomes point to a change in the way these students view the world. Regardless of the pedagogical approach utilized in expanding students' cultural horizons, the need to prepare more globally sensitive citizens can no longer be negotiated. Cultural competence and ability to participate responsibly in the global community is imperative for the achievement of a more harmonious and hopefully peaceful world.

The international study experience is especially important to the student in family science. The process of self-awareness and personal maturation prepares them for future work with families. Students' understanding of their own culture and how they fit into the world helps them as they examine the assumptions they have about cultural differences. Such knowledge aids in gaining respect for and sensitivity to the uniqueness of others.

In addition, family science students have the opportunity to recognize the universality of family problems around the world. Families everywhere experience similar situations in diverse contexts. The complexity of meeting the needs of diverse populations requires the family science graduate to be able to recognize similarities and differences among cultures. One way to accomplish this is through an international study experience.

REFERENCES

Banks, J. (1992). Multicultural education: Nature, challenges, and opportunities. In C. Diaz (Ed.), *Multicultural education for the 21st century* (pp. 23-37). Washington, DC: National Education Association.

Bennett, C. (1988). The effects of a multicultural education course on pre-service teachers' attitudes, knowledge, and behavior. Paper presented at the meeting of the American Educational Research Association. April, New Orleans.

Bochner, S. (1986). Coping with unfamiliar cultures: Adjustment or culture learning? *Australian Journal of Psychology, 38,* 347-358.

Bodger, D. (1998). Leisure, learning, and travel. *The Journal of Physical Education, Recreation, and Dance, 69,* 2-6.

Creswell, J. (1998). *Qualitative inquiry and research design: Choosing among five traditions.* Thousand Oaks, CA: Sage Publications.

Cross T., Bazron, B., Dennis, K., & Isaacs, M. (1989). Toward a culturally competent system of care (Vol.1). Washington, DC: Georgetown University.

Daloz, L. (1986). *Effective teaching and mentoring: Realizing the transformational power of adult learning experiences.* San Francisco, CA: Jossey-Bass.

Diaz, C. (1992). *Multicultural education for the 21st century.* Washington, DC: National Education Association.

Friedman, E. (1996). Received ideas and curriculum transformation. In E. Friedman, W. Kolmar, C. Flint, & P. Rothenberg (Eds.). *Creating an inclusive curriculum: A teaching sourcebook from the New Jersey Project* (pp. 1-9). New York: Teachers College Press.

Healy, L. (2001). *International social work: Professional action in an interdependent world.* New York: Oxford University Press.

Helms, J. (1995). An update of Helms's White and people of color racial identity models. In J. Ponterotto, J. Casas, L. Suzuki, & C. Alexander (Eds.) *Handbook of multicultural counseling,* (pp. 181-198). Thousand Oaks, CA: Sage.

Lum, D. (Ed.). (2003). Culturally competent practice: A framework for understanding diverse groups and justice issues (Second edition). Pacific Grove, CA: Thomson, Brooks/Cole.

Merzirow, J. (1991). *Transformative dimensions of adult learning.* San Francisco, CA: Jossey-Bass.

Moore, T. J. (1995). Assessment of multiculturalism: Life experience, personal attitudes, personal behavior, and professional behavior of teachers in one school district. Unpublished doctoral dissertation, University of Nebraska-Lincoln.

Oakes, J. & Lipton, M. (1999). *Teaching to change the world.* Boston: McGraw-Hill College.

Orlandi, M. A. (1992). The challenge of evaluating community-based prevention programs: A cross-cultural perspective. In M. A. Orlandi, R. Weston, & L. G. Epstein (Eds.), *Cultural competence for evaluators: A guide for alcohol and other drug abuse prevention practitioners working with ethnic/communities,* (pp. 1-22). Rockville, MD: U.S. Department of Health and Human Services, Office for Substance Abuse Prevention.

Strauss, A. & Corbin, J. (1990). *Basics of qualitative research: Grounded theory procedures and techniques.* Newbury Park, CA: Sage.

Washington, V. (1981). Impact of antiracism/multicultural education training on elementary teachers' attitudes and classroom behavior. *The Elementary School Journal, 81,* 186-192.

Winkelman, M. (1994). Cultural shock and adaptation. *Journal of Counseling and Development, 73:* 121-126.

Chapter 6

Global Ecology Instructional Model: An Application for the Study of Families in an International Context

Mozhdeh B. Bruss
Barbara J. Frazier
Eileen Buckley

In an age of global connectedness, the need for enabling increased awareness, tolerance, and cooperation skills is critical to a holistic higher education curriculum. Historically, undergraduate degree programs across the United States have offered students the opportunity to enroll in general education courses that expose them to multicultural and international issues. Beyond general education electives, a number of degree programs include multicultural and international topics as requirements for matriculation. Academic programs in family science typically include culture and gender courses and a growing number offer topics related to international issues and concerns.

BACKGROUND

Recognizing that only a select group of students have the opportunity to participate in study-abroad programs, it is important that international

The authors wish to acknowledge the Diether H. Haenicke Institute for International and Area Studies, and the International Committee of the College of Education for continued support of the globalization of teaching, scholarship, and service. In addition, the authors also wish to recognize the support of Dr. Linda Dannison, Chair of the Department of Family and Consumer Sciences, and Ms. Yatesha Robinson, graduate assistant in the Department of Family and Consumer Sciences.

doi:10.1300/5609_06

topics are brought into the classroom (American Council on Education, 2001). Furthermore, in academic environments in which a majority of the students are of one ethnic group, students may have limited access to ethnic and cultural diversity. The need for such courses becomes increasingly important especially in certain regions of the country. For instance, in fifteen of the twenty-four Midwestern public universities offering family and consumer sciences programs (College Board, 2002) the demographics of any one ethnic minority group did not exceed 10 percent of the total population enrolled (see Table 6.1).

Cushner and Mahon (2002) also emphasize the importance of international studies as a result of recent national events: "In response to the attacks of September 11, it has become increasingly evident that people need to understand far more about how others in the world live their lives and how they are perceived" (pp. 55-56). Although students may share this perspective, they may have fears that inhibit international travel, as indicated by a student in an international family and consumer sciences course: "I always wanted to travel around the world and learn new things, however, after 9/11—it felt much safer to stay in my bubble."

PURPOSE

The purpose of this chapter is to share a model of teaching about families in a global context, and to assist the infusion of such information/strategies in other family science curricula. The Global Ecology Instructional (GEI) model presented reflects the goals of the American Association of Family & Consumer Sciences (2001). It addresses the content of the National Council on Family Relations' content area, "Families in Society" for the Certified Family Life Educator designation. It is designed to engage students in the study of families and to increase their capacity to acquire and use knowledge and skills in building on assets of families globally. The authors draw on current theories and practices from different disciplines, such as sociology, psychology, biology, anthropology, education, economics, geography, and health to offer an integrated approach to the study of family.

TABLE 6.1. Student demographics for Midwestern public universities with more than 15,000 students (fall 2001).

University	Enroll-ment	White/Non-Hispanic (%)	10 percent and more of a certain ethnic group (%)
Family Studies Programs			
Bowling Green State University	15,517	88	
Central Michigan University	19,274	86	
Eastern Michigan University	18,322	68	22 Black/Non-Hispanic
Home Economics Programs			
Illinois State University	18,393	88	
Indiana University Bloomington	29,125	87	
Iowa State	23,060	85	
Kansas State University	18,612	88	
Kent State University	17,994	88	
Miami University: Oxford Campus	15,040	87	
Michigan State University	34,571	77	10 Black/Non-Hispanic
Northern Illinois University	17,445	65	18 Black/Non-Hispanic
Ohio State University: Columbus Campus	34,586	77	10 Black/Non-Hispanic
Ohio University	17,178	94	
Purdue University	30,568	85	
Southern Illinois University Carbondale	16,656	72	16 Black/Non-Hispanic
University of Akron	18,715	No data available	
University of Cincinnati	18,650	77	15 Black/Non-Hispanic
University of Illinois at Urbana-Champaign	27,744	66	13 Asian/Pacific Islanders
University of Minnesota: Twin Cities	27,699	80	
University of Missouri: Columbia	18,179	87	

TABLE 6.1 *(continued)*

University	Enroll-ment	White/Non-Hispanic (%)	10 percent and more of a certain ethnic group (%)
University of Nebraska—Lincoln	17,950	88	
Wayne State University	16,745	43	36 Black/Non-Hispanic
West Virginia University	16,121	91	
Western Michigan University	22,921	90	

Source: College Board, 2002. http://www.collegeboard.com/.

CONTEXT

The elements of the GEI model were developed and evaluated in two different courses taught over a three-year period. The courses, global study of food, family and culture, and global ecology of families, are offered through the Department of Family and Consumer Sciences. The first course is limited to twenty students and is open to upper-division undergraduate and graduate students. The latter, with a capacity of fifty students, is a general education course that also meets the requirements for students in family life education. Although both of these courses have been formally evaluated and specific findings from each have contributed to the development of the GEI model, student responses presented in this chapter are derived from the Global Study of Food, Family and Culture course (total N = 20). Qualitative methods were used to conduct content analysis of student assignments and evaluation results to identify themes that investigated successful elements of the GEI model (Patton, 1990). The case study research approach will be used to present the elements of the GEI model supported by direct quotations from the students (Stake, 1995). The Western Michigan University Human Subject Review Board approved the research proposal for use of student responses.

THEORETICAL FOUNDATIONS

The GEI model is grounded in concepts of human ecology (HE) theory that evolves from "the assumption that humans are a part of the total life system and cannot be considered apart from all other living species in nature and the environment that surrounds them" (Andrews, Bubolz, & Paolucci, 1980, p. 32). HE theory is based on a collection of assumptions that help to describe, explain, and predict family outcomes. The theory assumes that all parts of the environment are interrelated and influence one another. Families are a part of the total life system, so they are interdependent with the environment and other forms of life. Furthermore, the GEI model was based on the HE theory because, according to Bubolz & Sontag (1993),

> Human ecology principles must be more widely used as a basis for human action by professionals, policymakers, and citizens at large in order to achieve changes that are needed for human betterment, realization of universal values, and for improved quality of human life and quality of the environments, both locally and globally. (p. 443)

The GEI model presented in Figure 6.1 places the student at the center of the learning process. The model is intended to serve as a guide for developing courses that promote an ecological approach to the study of families in international settings. The GEI model developed by the authors is based on social cognitive theory (Bandura, 1986), which proposes that the continuous interaction of learners with the environment influences behavior change. Learning takes place via a complex, three-way relationship between learners, their environment, and the learners' self-efficacy. We use a series of activities, including student self-assessment, case study analysis, comparative and international family research demonstration projects, and a country-based research project to help students move toward cultural literacy and competence. Each activity was designed to promote positive learning outcomes related to knowledge, appreciation, and respect for diversity. Furthermore, because social cognitive theory emphasizes the concepts of self-efficacy and observational learning (Miller, Edwards, Kissling & Sanville, 2002), the GEI model was grounded on three critical elements, (1) research and evaluation, (2) cultural exposure, and (3) technology.

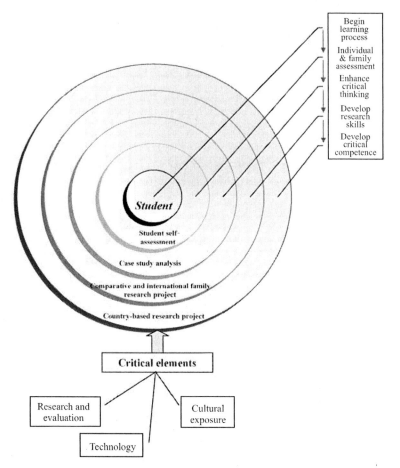

FIGURE 6.1. Global Ecology Instructional model.

LEARNING OBJECTIVES

The GEI model requires that students use critical thinking skills to

1. identify hidden biases that inhibit cross-cultural competency;
2. understand human ecology, family systems, and social construction theories as a theoretical framework that guides the study of families;
3. identify environmental and societal factors that influence their own family and cultural experience;

4. recognize environmental and societal factors that influence families across the globe;
5. develop an understanding of globalization; and
6. gain cross-cultural competency skills.

In addition, the use of the GEI model allows students to examine the following four questions:

1. How do environmental factors influence families in different countries and regions of the world?
2. How do media, education, religious beliefs, cultural values, and family systems influence families in different countries and regions around the world?
3. What are the unique structures, roles, strengths, and adaptive characteristics of families in different communities?
4. What beliefs, attitudes, and values individuate one family system from another in different parts of the world?

To achieve the learning objectives, students are provided with a theoretical foundation for the study of families along with knowledge of the different environmental and societal factors. For this, the instructor develops course presentations based on the literature using interactive media. In addition, students investigate different definitions of culture by various academic disciplines and develop their own definition. This strategy is useful in that certain topics, such as culture and family have different meaning to different people (Edwards & Neck, 2000). Students learn to look at families as a basic unit of community life in different countries and investigate the impact of different environmental and societal factors on the family in those societies. The overall learning objective for this model is to engage students in research, critical analysis, evaluation, and resynthesis of knowledge about families within the global community.

LEARNING ACTIVITIES

The success of the GEI model requires that students rapidly recognize the presence of hidden biases and their potential impact on investigation and reporting. During the first few weeks of class, students participate in a series of self-assessment activities that enable this process. These include

1. self-assessment of goals, objectives, and skills related to course content;
2. online Implicit Association Test (IAT);
3. critical thinking and hidden bias activity; and
4. Environmental Assessment Inventory.

Following the self-assessment activities students engage in three other learning activities. These include (1) case study analysis, (2) a comparative and international family research demonstration project, and (3) a country-based research project. In this section each of the self-assessment tools and learning activities, as elements of the GEI model, are described within the context of classes that were taught.

Self-Assessment of Goals, Objectives, and Skills

During the first day of class, students complete a self-assessment form that helps the instructor learn more about their goals and objectives related to the course. The assessment form is readministered with appropriate modification at the end of the semester to measure students' perception of their learning. In addition, the self-assessment form inventories frequency of Internet use and level of proficiency with technology. Specifically, students are asked to report perceived level of competence and comfort with computer and Internet use, online research, PowerPoint, and Web design. Early in the semester, the information aids the instructor in providing the necessary support to help students move beyond technical skill building and into the realm of content investigation and learning. See Table 6.2 for pre- and postdata on students' technical skills, an added benefit of this model.

Online Implicit Association Test (IAT)

The Implicit Association Test (IAT) is a set of widely used tests that are available on the Web (Tolerance.org, 2004). The IAT is designed to assess implicit associations between attributes and social groups identified by certain characteristics (Rudman, & Glick, 2001; McConnell, & Leibold, 2001). These include age (young and old), race (skin tones, Arab Muslims, etc.), body image (fat and thin), and

TABLE 6.2. Percentage of students reporting technical proficiency: pre- and postdata (*n* = 20).

	Precourse	Postcourse
Reported daily access and usage of Internet	17(85%)	19(95%)
Reported proficiency of Web design skills*	5(65%)	18(90%)
Reported proficiency of PowerPoint skills*	13(25%)	19(95%)
Reported proficiency of online research	17(85%)	20(100%)

Note: *p<.05 for McNemar's Tests (two-tailed)

others. The tests take approximately thirty minutes to complete. Each test uses judgment speed to measure the ease of association between certain social groups with words that have negative or positive notions. The IAT is a useful tool to introduce early in a class because it can provide students an opportunity to reflect on possible preferences for certain social groups. The Web site offers students background information on the test along with the option to discontinue the test if it makes them feel uncomfortable. Students are asked to access the Web site and learn more about the test before participating in it.

The IAT has been used in different settings. For instance, in a study of 389 health professionals specializing in obesity, IAT was administered along with a self-report questionnaire that obtained demographic information and explicit attitudes and experiences related to obesity. Based on the IAT results, researchers found a significant pro-thin and anti-fat implicit bias among the study participants (Schwartz, Chambliss, Brownell, Blair, & Billington, 2003).

Critical Thinking and Hidden Bias Activity

In the critical thinking and hidden bias activity, students learn and practice the steps in critical thinking (Chaffee, 1994), which involves

1. conscious desire and decision in developing beliefs,
2. use of reasonable and reflective thinking,
3. use of purposeful and self-regulatory judgment, and
4. basing judgment on well-defined explanations.

Students engage in a qualitative-based hidden bias activity, which enhances their understanding of their perceptions and attitudes. They analyze their perceptions and attitudes related to an unfamiliar country and identify potential factors associated with the development of these perceptions and attitudes. Specifically, students examine their knowledge, attitudes, and perceptions of the country under study through a series of open-ended questions. The Hidden Bias Activity for a discussion of Iran would be structured as follows:

I. Each student responds to the following questions:
   1. What is your perception of Iran?
   2. How do you feel about Iran?
   3. What do you know about Iran?
   4. What is the value of Iran to the world community?
II. Students will view a slide presentation of Iran.
III. Each student will respond to the following questions:
   1. What is your perception of Iran now?
   2. Did your perception of Iran change? Why?
   3. Did your attitude toward Iran change? Why?
   4. What factors have influenced your perception and attitude toward Iran?
IV. Group discussion.

At the end of the activity, students use a Likert scale (1-5 from strongly disagree to strongly agree) to measure the effectiveness of the activity. Through this exercise students learn to use qualitative and quantitative research methods in data collection and reporting, which can enhance their investigative skills (Edwards & Neck, 2000). In addition, it can facilitate learning about different cultures, as reported by one student who participated in this activity:

> This activity helped me realize that I know very little about other cultures in comparison to what I think I know. I have preformed assumptions that are probably incorrect based on media and interpretations of partial bits of information.

Environmental Assessment Inventory (EAI)

Following a thorough study of the theoretical frameworks used for the study of families, which are human ecology (Andrews, et al.

1980), family systems (Bowen, 1978), and social construction (Coltrane, 1998) theories, students use the Environmental Assessment Inventory (EAI) form, which was especially designed for this model. The EAI allows students to use qualitative and quantitative questions to investigate the influence of ten different environmental and societal factors on their own family's experience (Figure 6.2). These factors include

1. media and technology,
2. education,
3. socioeconomic status,
4. ethnicity,
5. religious belief and practice,
6. urban and/or rural dwelling,
7. disease and health status, and
8. food beliefs, attitudes and practices.

In this activity, students use a constructivist approach (Coltrane, 1998) to explore and rate the impact of each factor on their family, making meaning of their family experience. They use human ecology theory (Andrews, et al., 1980) and family systems theory (Bowen, 1978) to examine ways in which their families maintained and improved individual and collective well-being by seeking health, education, and learning, relationships, productive work, experiences, and symbolic systems that sustained meaning and a sense of community. EAI helps students determine how their families are influenced and affected by environmental and societal factors. In addition, this assignment obtains baseline information on students' attitudes toward and experiences with the factors.

Case Study Analysis

Building on the theoretical framework used for the study of families, students learn to examine environmental and societal factors influencing families through a set of case studies from around the world. Prior to the use of these case studies, students are offered an overview of human geography to help facilitate the global study of the subject matter. Human geography is the study of people in different

Environmental Assessment Inventory Form   Name: _ _ _ _ _ _ _ _ _

1. Rate the degree to which each of the factors below has influenced your family experience.
2. Write a brief explanation with at least two specific examples of how each factor influenced your family experience.
3. If a factor is rated as not significant, explain why it has not influenced your family experience.
4. Finally, discuss what you have learned from this assessment and how you plan to use this learning experience to teach others.

For each factor please circle your response (a number) and provide an explanation.

FIGURE 6.2. Environmental Assessment Inventory Form.

countries and regions. Students can use the human geography template (Figure 6.3) to examine the following elements:

1. spatial terms that help pinpoint locations,
2. placement in the world and its regions,
3. physical systems,
4. human systems,
5. environment and society, and
6. geographic history.

	Human geography elements	Description	How might a family interact in this element?
1	Spatial terms that help us pinpoint locations	*In this space,* provide the absolute location of this country (using latitude and longitude).	*In this space,* describe how the location of this country influences the family.
2	Placement in the world and its regions	*In this space,* describe the physical space and what it looks like (physical surroundings and environmental features).	*In this space,* describe the impact of the country's geographic placement in the world on the families. These may include economics, food, religious significance, etc.
3	Physical systems	*In this space,* describe the physical makeup of the area (land, water, and atmosphere).	*In this space,* describe the family's interaction with land, water, and atmosphere in this country.
4	Human systems	*In this space,* describe how people have historically interacted with the land (developing the land, building infrastructure, etc.).	*In this space,* describe how families today interact with the human systems of land development and building infrastructure.
5	Environment and society	*In this space,* describe how people interact with the environment and how the environment interacts with people. (Natural disasters, effects on the environment, etc.).	*In this space,* describe the family's interaction with different environmental factors.
6	Geographic history	*In this space,* briefly describe the geographic history of the country.	*In this space,* describe how geographic history has influenced the family.

FIGURE 6.3. Human Geography Elements template.

Case studies humanize the subject matter. Moreover, it helps to develop skills in team learning, reporting, and critical thinking. Case studies present a set of events within a real-life context and are a valuable way to share the experiences of others. They are also useful for encouraging discussion about best practices and problem-solving strategies. The authors were unable to locate published case studies focusing on international family issues, so a series of case studies were created for use in the course. Case studies were developed to emphasize the effects of key environmental and societal factors, such as media, technology, education, religion, political and economic systems, and culture, on families in different parts of the world. For example, one case study focuses on a Bolivian family who is about to move from a rural community to an urban area to take jobs in apparel manufacturing. The case study provides cultural, economic, social, and political background on Bolivia, and describes the lifestyle of a typical rural Bolivian family. Students are asked to read the case study in preparation for class discussion. The case study includes discussion questions, for which students must prepare responses prior to class. The Bolivian case study offers opportunities to discuss several issues, including positive and negative aspects of economic development activities in poor countries, the role of foreign manufacturers in improving the well-being of workers, and the effect of national and international policies on families.

Comparative and International Family Research Demonstration Project

Students examine the influence of culture on individuals and families with regard to body image, health beliefs, food choices, gender roles, and other beliefs, values, and practices. They come to understand that when a group of people coexist in an environment they establish norms and standards to govern behavior. In order to study the distinct characteristics of any one group, students use a constructivist approach (Coltrane, 1998), which supports the use of both quantitative and qualitative methods in studying families' perception, knowledge, attitudes, and practices in different international settings. More specifically, students are introduced to quantitative methods, which include survey instruments and sociocultural inventory constructs developed to measure perceptions, beliefs, attitudes, and practices of individuals, families, and communities (Krathwohl, 1998). They are also familiarized with qualitative methods such as ethnography, map making, kinship analysis, participant observation, and interviews/ focus groups (Bogdan & Biklen, 1998).

Following this introductory study of research methods, students engage in a demonstration project which requires that they convey to others well-researched information about issues related to family in the context of culture. They learn to identify and describe the environmental and societal factors and their influences on the overall family experience of individuals in different societies. The activity requires that students either engage in a one-on-one interview with someone who has lived more than half of his or her life in another country or to conduct a literature review of a country. In both of these instances, the students use a constructivist approach by formulating both open- and closed-ended research questions to examine the influence of a series of environmental and societal factors on the individual's family. These factors include, but are not limited to, religion, education, mass media, sociocultural beliefs and values, economics, sociopolitical issues, meals and food preference, access and use of health care, housing and geographic location. Students are required to research and report their findings to the class.

Country-Based Research Project

Prior to the introduction of the country-based research project, the entire class engages in an online-based comparative and critical analysis of the environmental and societal factors in two different countries. Students are given the option to either use the two countries selected for comparison by the instructor or choose two others that adequately offer information to engage them in this process. Focusing on each environmental and societal factor, students are asked to research a set of open-ended questions. For instance, in regard to "health care situation, access and utilization by families," students are asked to use a set of health-related questions to research two countries. Sample questions include:

1. rates of malnutrition, infant mortality, child mortality, and maternal mortality for the two countries;

2. factors contributing to the difference in the malnutrition rates for each country;
3. main differences between the countries health care systems; and
4. factors that have influenced the difference in the disease pattern between the two countries.

Students may use the interactive page on the class Web site to post their responses to the comparative open-ended questions or prepare a written response that can be shared in class. In using the class Web site, students have the opportunity to read others' responses to the same questions. Effective application of this activity requires that students use critical thinking skills (Chaffee, 1994) to develop and convey well-thought-out responses that are accurate and factual. This activity is designed to enhance critical thinking, help understand the issues related to each topic, and prepare students for reporting findings on their country. One student reflected on this activity.

> The country comparative questions were helpful in improving my analytical skills. I now feel that I am much more able to critically evaluate the concepts and I think that this class has helped me hone my critical thinking skills as well.

Following the initial developmental exploration and reflection, students are invited to select a country that they will study through the semester. Students may select their countries for various reasons such as previous travel experience to the country, an upcoming study-abroad course, curiosity, interest in a region, and country of ancestry. This research-based activity requires that students use peer-reviewed literature to examine the following ten aspects of a country in regard to families.

1. Elements of human geography in relation to families.
2. Sociocultural beliefs, values, and practices of families including ethnic makeup of the society.
3. Influence of sociopolitical systems and structures on family well-being.
4. Food accessibility, dietary habits, food beliefs and values, and body image by the families.

5. Economic status and conditions of the country and the families.
6. Technological resources within the country and their influence on families.
7. Health care situation, access, and utilization by the families.
8. Religious beliefs and practices among families.
9. Impact of globalization on the families and sustainable development activities in the country.
10. Domestic and international migration patterns among families.

During each class session, one of the topics is the subject of discussion in the class. The format used for presenting the research information requires that students create and weekly update Web pages focusing on their assigned country. Specifically, during each class session, following an overview presentation of the topic by the instructor, the students' Web pages are displayed on the overhead screen, while each student presents the findings related to his or her specific country. Previous experience with this activity has demonstrated that the discussions tend to be rich with information, as reflected in this student's comment: "I learned a great deal about not only the country I researched but about other countries around the world. I also developed a greater appreciation for the world around me and I have more of an open mind."

The comparative analysis of the issues between countries helps students see the commonality and diversity of families in the global community. Although students rely mainly on peer-reviewed journal articles and published books, they can supplement their research with information from other sources, such as government and nongovernment Web sites. In the context of building their Web sites, students are advised to be aware of their hidden biases and to report information in an objective manner. Instructor review of Web sites from a recently completed course indicated that most students were sensitive to presenting the information in a factual and objective manner. In some cases, although students may have disagreed with certain cultural practices such as the caste system or genital mutilation, they objectively presented information on the practice without passing personal judgment.

Learning this higher-level thinking and acceptance for those who are different than oneself is critical to effectively working in a globally connected society. Specifically, this process requires an understanding of the differences in families and their unique ways of interpreting particular events. According to Arms, Davidson, & Moore (1992) the objective of such courses is to gain knowledge, understanding, and insight into the reality that families face in different communities and what that reality means as it plays out in today's interdependent global village. Students who are exposed to this learning in higher education may be better equipped to critically analyze the world around them and more effectively contribute to the workforce. This investigative and reporting approach to learning was found to be highly effective in moving students through the different levels of thinking, as stated by one student:

> I learned many things and had some interesting experiences. I was taken by surprise at the differences the various countries had with each other and yet all shared a common thread: culture. Each country, region, town, family, has its own unique and individualized culture that helps it to create meaning. Learning about those different cultures has been very interesting and sometimes, hard to accept because they are so very different than my own culture.

CRITICAL ELEMENTS OF THE GEI MODEL

The GEI model is grounded in three critical elements, (1) research and evaluation, (2) cultural exposure, and (3) technology. In addition, other considerations with regard to these three critical elements are highlighted in this section.

Research and Evaluation

The evaluative and research aspect of this model engages students in a series of qualitative and quantitative-based research and evaluation activities. For instance, the hidden bias activity helps students develop qualitative research skills, while the pre- and postassessment tool offers students the opportunity to self-evaluate technical skills and learning outcomes. In addition to the different learning activities, students use an instructor-prepared evaluation tool to conduct peer evaluation of the Web pages designed for the country-based research project. The evaluative element of the GEI model also engages the instructor in conducting ongoing evaluation of students through classroom observation, discussion, summary of peer-reviewed research findings, and Web page submissions. In addition, the instructor uses data from the pre- and postassessment form to evaluate the course for its effectiveness in presenting the ecological model. One such question asks students to rate the importance of the knowledge of different environmental and societal factors in helping them with their understanding of families in a country. Analysis of the results from the pre- and postassessment is used by the instructor to further develop the course content. Students are also asked to qualitatively evaluate the use of these factors in their understanding of issues related to families in international settings. Because the GEI model intends to help students examine the impact of different environmental and societal factors on families, seeking student feedback and conducting content analyses of responses support the use of the model. This is evidenced in one student's remark:

> Before this class, I would have tried to find simple answers to hard questions; however, I have learned that to adequately understand how or why something "is" you must understand all factors that contribute to that thing. Before this class, I could not adequately identify these factors. These factors maybe due to the practices of man, such as religion and government, or be to the inherent layout of the country, such as geography and climate. All of these factors I now recognize as part of the whole picture.

Cultural Exposure

Another important element critical to the effectiveness of the GEI model is cultural exposure. In addition to the cultural exposure gained as a result of engaging in different learning activities, students are also exposed to people of different countries and the sharing of their stories. Guest speakers from different countries are invited to class and foreign films are also included in the curriculum. International students may be invited to present their own personal experiences. For instance, in one class, a panel included a student from the

Ivory Coast and a couple from Mainland China. Speakers were asked to share their familial experiences within the context of the economic development of their country. On another occasion, a Pakistani student spoke about her personal cultural interaction with courting and marriage. Foreign films and cultural documentaries may also enhance student experiences especially when presenting cultures that are less familiar to the students. One student reflected that, "The guest speakers and videos really contributed to my learning experience."

Technology

A third critical element of this model is technology, which is imbedded in a number of learning activities. To ensure positive learning outcomes, students are offered skill-building activities in Web design using programs such as Netscape, which is relatively user friendly. In addition, students are also instructed in other aspects of technology-based projects, which include,

1. identifying the target audience for the final Web site;
2. the role and responsibility of the Web designer as to the sensitive presentation of the content;
3. copyright laws regarding use of images and other materials from the Web;
4. interactive design considerations; and
5. appropriate presentation of the researched materials.

MODEL OUTCOMES

Cultural Competence: Knowledge, Appreciation, and Respect

Typically, multicultural courses aim to increase awareness and tolerance with regard to diversity of cultures. Although the GEI model intends to increase awareness through cultural literacy, it is also designed to help students achieve appreciation and respect for diverse cultures of the world. To ensure that students have achieved the content-based learning outcomes, a written examination that measures knowledge of the subject matter is administered. In addition, a final assessment is conducted by the instructor, which includes the use of a rubric to score students' Web page projects for inclusion of adequate and relevant research information and quality and accuracy of materials presented. With regard to the attitudinal learning outcomes of appreciation and respect, students are engaged in a final exercise that offers them the opportunity to evaluate their overall learning experience: they send an e-mail to the instructor reflecting on the *lessons learned,* the *highlights,* and the *challenges* of their learning experience. Content analysis of the e-mails suggests that most students reported personal learning and growth with regard to the intended outcomes of cultural awareness, appreciation, and respect. One student commented:

> Wow, I have learned so much, I'm not sure if I can put it all into words. I think the most significant thing I got out of this whole experience was an appreciation for cultures that are different than my own. I don't even know if appreciation is a strong enough word. I think now I am hooked on indulging myself into other cultures. I just want to experience every single one. Just so that I can feel what makes other people happy, sad, what makes them get up in the morning, and [what] they think of as they go to sleep. How their lives are different than mine and what things we all share. As I experienced these different cultures I realized I am just an outsider, and probably always will be to them. That was hard to accept, that I couldn't dig as deep as I wanted to on my own, I need other people's help. The only way to really get inside the culture is by talking to its people while experiencing it first-hand. That's what I've learned, and I'm thrilled about it. I appreciate my family and my culture even more than I ever have before, but that doesn't stop me from wanting to travel again as soon as possible!! Thanks for the wonderful experience.

Application of the Model

According to the American Council on Education (2000), "America's future depends on our ability to develop a citizenry that is globally competent. Our nation's place in the world will be determined by our society, whether it is internationally competent, comfortable and confident" (p. 5). A key mission of family science programs is to prepare students to function as globally competent members of the workforce. This model has the potential for inclusion into family science curricula, especially for students who may not have access to study-abroad opportunities. It could also be used to prepare those students who may choose to participate in a study-abroad experience. One student remarked, "By researching this country, I feel more comfortable about studying abroad there, because my plan is to go there next year." The use of this model requires a strong commitment from the students. They are expected to work hard in pursuit of their knowledge and the presentation of their findings. Although students are well aware of this expectation, they learn to appreciate the learning style created by this model. Another student stated, "If all of my classes were like this one, I would never stop going to school."

The model allows for flexibility and revisions. However, students should be encouraged to select both Western and non-Western cultures of the world for their study, as indicated by one student, "I especially enjoyed being exposed to other cultures than Western ones." The diverse research and reporting will enhance classroom discussion and student appreciation for the diversity of families around the globe. One student indicated, "I learned about others and myself and got a better grasp of the world around me. I feel more 'global' and accepting." Finally, the ecological aspect of this model allows students to study the influence and relationship of different environmental and societal factors on families in a specific country. Students can gain the necessary analytical tools to conduct similar studies on other countries. This was clearly evident in another student comment:

> It is great to have each student identify with a specific country because by doing that they are not only learning a lot about that one country but also learning how to analyze another country if they would like to learn more. Plus since we shared our information in class we were able to make comparisons with these other countries and see how similar or different our countries are. Learning about the social-political structure, family life, agriculture, etc., and how they are all intertwined, so that one of these concepts can build off of the other is very helpful in building information on the countries.

In summary, there is need for teaching practices that help larger numbers of undergraduate students to reach higher-level thinking (Quoss, Williams & Cooney, 2000). The GEI model supports student use of research methods to advance through a process that facilitates higher-level evaluative and relativist thinking. The diagnostic research skills gained from this model aid students in better understanding community structures and processes with impact on families. In addition, the model provides a creative and practical approach to engaging students in learning about global issues that affect families. Students learn to apply concepts gained from this model to future work with families in both national and international settings and increase their sensitivity to global issues. A student summed it up: "Our world is constantly struggling with many issues, and for me to realize this, or may be more concerned [with] is why I will always value what has been taught and pointed out to me forever."

REFERENCES

American Association of Family and Consumer Sciences (2001). FCS Backgrounder: Essence of Family & Consumer Sciences—adapted from the AAFCS 2001 Annual Meeting Keynote Address "The Essence of Our Being." Retrieved June 1, 2004, from http://www.aafcs.org/resources/mediatoolkit .html.

American Council on Education (ACE) (2000). Expanding the international scope of Universities: A strategic vision statement for learning, scholarship and engagement in the New Century National Association of State Universities and Land-Grant Colleges. Retrieved June 1, 2004, from http://www.nasulgc.org/publications/Visions.pdf.

American Council on Education (ACE) (2001). ACE reports suggest a decline in U.S. college and university international education despite public interest. Retrieved August 25, 2003, from http://www.acenet.edu/news/press_release/2001/11November/ford_intl_rept.html. (Article no longer available.)

Andrews, M. P., Bubolz, M. M., & Paolucci, B. (1980). An ecological approach to study of the family. *Marriage and Family Review, 3,* 29-49.

Arms, K., Davidson, J., & Moore, N. (1992). *Cultural diversity and families.* Dubuque, IA: Brown & Benchmark.

Bandura, A. (1986). *Social foundations of thought and action: A social cognitive theory.* Englewood Cliffs, NJ: Prentice-Hall.

Bogdan, R. C. & Biklen, S. K. (1998). *Qualitative research for education: An introduction to theory and methods* (Third edition). Boston: Allyn and Bacon.

Bowen M. (1978). *Family therapy in clinical practice.* New York: Aronson.

Bubolz, M. M. & Sontag, S. M. (1993). Human ecology theory. In P. G. Boss, W. J. Doherty, R. LaRossa, W. R. Schumm, & S.K. Steinmetz (Eds.), *Sourcebook of family theories and methods: A contextual approach* (pp. 419-444). New York: Plenum Press.

Chaffee, J. (1994). *Thinking critically* (Fourth edition). Boston: Houghton Mifflin.

College Board. (2002). Retrieved August 25, 2003, from http://www.collegeboard .com.

Coltrane, S. (1998). *Gender and families.* Thousand Oaks, CA: Pine Forge Press.

Cushner, K. & Mahon, J. (2002). Overseas student teaching: Affecting personal, professional, and global competencies in an age of globalization. *Journal of Studies in International Education, 6* (1), 44-58.

Edwards, T.M. & Neck, C.P. (2000). The I-MAC teaching model for beginning family science instructors. *Family Science Review, 13* (1-2), 14-30.

Krathwohl, D. R. (1998). *Methods of educational and social science research: An integrated approach* (Second edition). New York: Longman.

McConnell, A. R. & Leibold, J. M. (2001). Relations among the implicit association test, discriminatory behavior, and explicit measures of racial attitudes. *Journal of Experimental Social Psychology, 37,* 435-442.

Miller, C. K., Edwards, L., Kissling, G., Sanville, L. (2002). Evaluation of a theory-based nutrition intervention for older adults with diabetes mellitus. *Journal of the American Dietetic Association, 102,* 1069-1074, 1079-1081.

Patton, M. Q. (1990). *Qualitative evaluation and research methods* (Second edition) Newbury Park, CA: Sage Publications.

Quoss, B., Williams K.C., & Cooney, M. (2000). Promoting students' intellectual development: A qualitative study of teaching practices. *Family Science Review, 13* (1-2), 31-43.

Rudman, L. A. & Glick, P. (2001). Prescriptive gender stereotypes and backlash toward agentic women. *Journal of Social Issue, 57,* 743-762.

Schwartz, M. B., Chambliss, H. O., Brownell, K. D., Blair, S. N., & Billington, C. (2003). Weight bias among health professionals specializing in obesity. *Obesity Research, 11*(9), 1033-1039.

Stake, R.E. (1995). *The art of case study research.* Thousand Oaks, CA: Sage Publications.

Tolerance.org. (2004). The Southern Poverty Law Center. Retrieved June 1, 2004, from http://www.tolerance.org/hidden_bias/index.html.

Chapter 7

The Fulbright Programs Model for Teaching and Learning About International Families

María E. Canabal

Family educators acknowledge the need for international education in colleges and universities (Andrews, 2003; Crowford, 1993; Firebaugh & Deacon, 1990; Paige & Williams, 2001). Many have recommended the globalization of the curriculum for decades as a means to prepare students for the challenges of an increasing global interdependence (Andrews, 2000; Andrews, 2003; Firebaugh & Miller, 2000; Hanvey, 1979; Harari, 1981; Kameoka, 1996). Anderson (2003) defines global interdependence as "valuing the interconnectedness and mutually dependent parts in creative ways to address the complex issues of families, communities and countries" (p. iii). Furthermore, Tucker (2003) believes that "functioning successfully in a global community is now a requirement" for family oriented professionals (p. 3). However, despite the efforts of some higher education units in globalizing the curriculum, Paige and Williams (2001) report that in their study of students' perceptions, "the majority of the students feel unprepared to participate in a global society in both their professional and their personal lives" (p. 82).

The challenge often times is that faculty members do not feel confident discussing international family issues when they have not been exposed to multicultural experiences themselves. Faculty interaction with families and individuals from other countries is one way to solve or alleviate this situation. Several private and government sponsored programs provide opportunities for faculty and students to have a di-

doi:10.1300/5609_07   *125*

rect exposure to other cultures. The well-known Fulbright Program
offers one such opportunity.

In 1946, the United States Congress created the Fulbright Program
sponsored by Senator J. William Fulbright "to increase mutual understanding between the people of the United States and other countries
through the exchange of persons, knowledge and skills" Institute for
International Education (IIE) (2004). The program is funded by the
U.S. Department of State, Bureau of Educational and Cultural Affairs
(BECA) and administered by the Council for International Exchange
of Scholars (CIES), a private, nonprofit organization. According to a
2002 evaluation of the program by the Stanford Research Institute
(SRI), 73 percent of the returning scholars "have incorporated aspects of their Fulbright experience into courses and teaching methods" (Gomes & Mallonee, 2002; CIES, 2004).

In this chapter, experiences with two programs under the Fulbright
umbrella are discussed: (1) The traditional U.S. Fulbright Scholar
Program, which is designed for American college and university faculty, professionals, and independent scholars to lecture and conduct
research in a wide variety of academic disciplines, and, (2) the Educational Partnerships Program, which provides opportunities to establish linkages between U.S. and foreign academic institutions (BECA,
2003). The purpose of this chapter is to illustrate ways in which family science faculty can increase their knowledge about families from
other cultures. This familiarity will provide the confidence needed to
incorporate multicultural content into the curriculum.

FULBRIGHT SCHOLAR PROGRAM

In the summer of 1995, I was awarded a fellowship to spend five
months as a Senior Fulbright Scholar at the Avinashilingam Institute
for Home Sciences and Higher Education for Women (Deemed University) located in the city of Coimbatore, Tamil Nadu in South India.
This is an all-woman, residential institution that follows Ghandian
philosophy and values. During my assignment, I taught a family resource management course to graduate students and collected data
related to various resource management and consumer-related topics
such as values, attitudes toward money, decision making, and the
conflict between work and family. In addition to my teaching and research duties, I had the opportunity to meet with and deliver numer-

ous presentations to various groups in the communities such as consumer advocacy groups, Rotary clubs, faculty and students from
other institutions, and teachers in training. Some of the topics of the
presentations included: The Conflict Between Work and Family and
the Management of Time; The Economic Value of Women's Unpaid
Work; Components of Consumer Education in the United States; The
Application of the Systems Approach to Family Resource Management in Teaching and Research; Consumer Rights and Responsibilities in a Market Economy; The Consumer Movement in the United
States; Management of Stress; and Barriers to Harmony Among Nations and Individuals. I also traveled to other places in India, from big
cities to remote, rural areas.

The discussions with my students about Indian and U.S. families
in and out of the classroom were fascinating for both of us. We talked
about several family related topics such as: arranged marriages, dowry-
related issues, age at marriage, number of children per family, child
gender preferences, female infanticide, child labor, family policies,
care of the elderly, rural versus urban family traditions, gender
division of household labor, and women's issues, among others. For
example, students explained that an arranged marriage is very natural
and acceptable. It was very difficult for them to imagine what it
would be like to date and to choose their own partner. In their eyes
such activity, without parents' intervention, seems very risky. They
also explained how traditions such as dowry have been legally ban-
ned, but still continue as a common practice.

We followed the ecosystems approach as a framework for discussion
and for field investigation of family resource management topics. By
choosing this framework, we were able to identify the interaction
among the different systems such as religion, government, business,
and social systems affecting and being affected by the family system.
By looking at commonalities and differences among groups within
the Indian population and the United States, the effect of culture on
our decisions as individuals and as families became evident.

Besides the classroom activities, Avinashilingam University has a
very strong outreach program in which all students, regardless of major, must provide service to the community. That gave me the opportunity to visit remote, rural villages and inner-city families and learn
about their resources (or lack thereof), traditions, values, and differences based on socioeconomic status, caste, religion, region of the

country from which they originate, practices in rearing children, and the effect of public policy on families. I also had the opportunity to visit and interact with the families of my students, my colleagues, university administrators, and elite government and business leaders in various communities, which provided a broader picture of families in India. These visits and observations were essential in the classroom discussion of families as ecosystems.

Upon my return to the United States, I was able to incorporate what I learned during my Fulbright experience into the courses I teach at Illinois State University. Incorporating international issues in class is more interesting when you have experienced them firsthand and can then discuss real cases/scenarios to illustrate a point. For example, I felt more confident explaining how culture, religion, and family values influence consumers' resource management styles and decisions by using real-life vignettes from India and other cultures.

My inclusion of these experiences in my lectures and discussions motivated students in the United States to interact with my students in India. Some of them started corresponding and, through the Human Services Organization, Illinois State University (ISU) students collected and sent books and research journals on family and consumer sciences related topics for the library in Avinashilingam.

The contacts I established during my first visit to India, coupled with a better understanding of the problems faced by families and individuals as consumers in India and the United States, provided the bases for a successful grant proposal for an Educational Partnership Program, another Fulbright Program, involving several faculty members from both countries. This program allowed me to visit India several times and to address consumer and gender-related issues identified by my students and colleagues during the first visit.

FULBRIGHT EDUCATIONAL PARTNERSHIP PROGRAM

This project consisted of a three-year faculty exchange program between Illinois State University and Avinashilingam University (Coimbatore, South India) designed to promote democracy and human rights by acknowledging the importance of informed, actively involved families and individuals as consumers/citizens. The program included teaching, faculty development, and outreach activities for the enrichment and understanding of participatory government by enhancing the knowledge and skills necessary for their involvement in free enterprise, and democratic processes. A better understanding of the consumer's role in democracy and the Indian free market economy is expected to empower Indian families and individuals to become more active participants in the political and economic decisions that affect them and their society.

The faculty members from Illinois State University who participated in the program increased their understanding and appreciation of Indian society, as well as the growing role of India in the world economy. As a result of this exchange, these faculty members are in a better position to revise and improve the curriculum in areas such as non-Western cultures, acceptance of diversity, and international studies.

The scope of the project was multidisciplinary in nature, involving faculty from different fields of study such as political science, family and consumer sciences, women's studies, philosophy, education, and nursing. Sixteen faculty members were invited to participate in this program. (The participation was as follows: 1998—three from India and three from ISU; 1999—two from India and two from ISU; 2000—three from India and three from ISU. As director of the program I visited India in 1998 and in 2000.) Their visit to the host institution ranged from one to three months. They participated in various educational and cultural programs within the universities and the communities in which they were located. The objectives of the project included:

1. Establish a computer link between both institutions to facilitate faculty and students' communication and exchange of materials and ideas over time.
2. Expand information related to non-Western culture and values in selected general education courses at Illinois State University by providing an opportunity for faculty to travel and study in India and to gather material and information for course development or revision.
3. Strengthen Illinois State University programs and consumer-related courses by providing an opportunity for involved faculty to study in India and develop materials to be implemented across the curriculum.
4. Provide Indian faculty with an opportunity to develop understanding and pedagogical materials in areas such as the role of

women and consumers in a democratic society, so that these
topics may be integrated in their courses across the curriculum.
5. Develop outreach educational programs to empower Indian
women and consumers to fully participate in the changing Indian economic life.

The program was intended to create a self-sustaining relationship
between the two institutions to ensure increased globalization and
democratic understanding among the faculty members.

Program Implementation

A total of sixteen faculty members from both institutions participated in the actual exchange program from 1998 to 2000. Their visits
to the host institution provided these individuals the opportunity to
interact with other faculty, students, and communities, thus increasing the number of people actually benefiting from the program. The
participating faculty from India gathered materials, interviewed faculty, attended classes, and participated in seminars and lectures in
their areas of interest. They also interacted with families in the communities. The visiting faculty from Illinois State University engaged
in similar activities in India. They were particularly interested in the
successful outreach programs of Avinashilingam University.

Upon the completion of their visits, each participating faculty
member was required to provide an evaluation of the experience using the Participants Report in the Appendix. This form is an adaptation of the form Fulbright grantees use after completing their assignments. The quotes for this chapter were selected from Part II of their
reports. The quotes illustrate the nature and impact of the exchange
program on the participants and on their academic duties. The quotes
offer a glimpse into the benefits of the experience. Participants' comments are presented by institution: Illinois State University and
Avinashilingam University, respectively.

Participants from Illinois State University

One faculty member commented on the interaction he had with
faculty and students in India. He reflected on the pedagogical impact
this experience will have in a course he teaches at ISU:

My many discussions with faculty and students concerning North American feminism and the sexual politics of contemporary Indian society will prove immensely valuable in my teaching in women's studies at Illinois State University . . . I return to ISU with many concrete examples of those differences, of ways in which oppression shows very different faces in different cultural settings. Being able to use those examples in the classroom will make a profound difference to the effectiveness of my teaching on this important subject.

Similarly, a participant further identified, in more concrete terms, how she plans to incorporate changes in her class based on what she learned from the experience:

This experience will forever change the way I teach women's studies . . . I have come to realize that perhaps the best way to teach students about gender equality and democracy is to start with cultures and groups that understand women's economic empowerment at the basic grassroots level and then work up to some of the more complex theoretical issues. I've also come to realize the importance of empowering women as consumers to democratic projects: a dimension to women empowerment that my philosophical training had not made visible to me. . . . As a result of my interactions with students and faculty at Avinashilingam University, I plan to restructure my Gender, Women, and Society course so that I frame women's issues in a way more sensitive to cultural differences between women outside the United States.

Another participant valued the transformation that her exposure to a different culture caused in her. She also commented on the value of sharing the experience with colleagues from her institution:

This experience has become the most inspiring, self-transforming experience of my life. The Indian people I had the opportunity to meet shared with me the many beautiful secrets of the Indian culture. It was a privilege to have this experience and to be in the company of my ISU faculty colleagues.

An ISU faculty member involved in the education of future nurses reflected on how her visit to India increased her understanding of the condition of women in this country and the challenges faced by these professionals in less-developed nations. Even though she refers to the nursing profession, her comments are also valuable for family science faculty as they apply to such topics as pregnancy, nutrition, and women's education:

> Professionally, this experience helped me gain an understanding of the role and value of education for women in India, the status of Indian nursing education and nutritional status of pregnant women in India. I am better able to understand the obstacles and opportunities encountered when starting a health care program in a developing nation.

Participants from Avinashilingam University

Participants from Avinashilingam University were more specific about their accomplishments during their visit to ISU. Through their comments we can also identify their contributions in the classroom and infer the impact of their presence on ISU students and faculty. They also provided details of the professional activities attended and their participation in the community:

> I presented a paper at the American Council on Consumer Interests. In almost all classes I participated in the discussion of topics. I also explained the Indian situation on the respective issues raised by students. I gave a lecture and presented a videotape about the family styles in India and the celebrations for the girl child at different stages in her life. I also interacted and exchanged ideas in the research symposium, seminars, and conferences.

An Indian participant compared the situation of women in the United States to those in her country, recognizing her role as an educator in the empowerment of women in India:

> Empowerment of women in the United States in all walks of life is incomparable with women in my country. We have to put in greater efforts to achieve this. Classroom presentations, seminars, conferences, and meetings enlightened us on women[s] issues.

Not all comments were related to the classroom or academic experiences. Their interaction with the community and their cultural and educational visits also contributed to their appreciation of the program:

> Visits to the Bloomington-Normal and Springfield communities were a great learning experience on different stores and facilities, libraries, [Abraham] Lincoln life, etc. Visits to Diet Counseling Center at school lunch programs, Student Health Center, and community extension centers gave me a better perspective of their programs.

In talking about her experience using technology in the classroom, the same participant said:

> It was a delightful experience. I have just started using this technology, but a lot more needs to be learned to become familiar with the same. I think that after reaching my home country I will be able to practice a lot more.

Finally, Indian participants summarized and evaluated their participation in the exchange programs:

> On the whole our visit was successful. We could observe and learn a lot with regard to the area of specialization as well as other areas of interest. I am fully satisfied with my visit to ISU. I have accomplished the objectives with which I had come and have also much more knowledge and information. I have collected lots of materials and information to be shared with faculty and students and the community at large.

For another:

> I had a very good relationship with faculty and shared lots of information both academic and nonacademic. I developed friendly relationships; discussed course content; discussed methods of evaluation, grading, and evaluating students, examinations, etc.; collected information and materials from faculty; identified examiners; discussed the varied aspects of women[s] issues, such as their role in the home, stress, violence, problems, ways of overcoming problems both at home and at work, etc.; analyzed

facts related to U.S.A. and India. I visited the homes of faculty and people of the local community; made friends; attended community functions; visited places . . . to understand many aspects related to work, food habits, health, buying habits, etc.

Since the development of the program, several faculty members from ISU have agreed to serve as external reviewers for faculty members in Avinashilingam who are working on their doctoral dissertations. Faculty from both institutions are also collaborating on research. In addition, some students from Avinashilingam University have been admitted to graduate programs at ISU. This illustrates the commitment of both institutions and highlights the continued interaction among faculty and students beyond this project.

DISCUSSION AND RECOMMENDATIONS

Family science instructors have always recognized the importance of cultural frameworks in the study of topics such as courtship and marriage, child care, gender roles, parental involvement, and resource management, among others. Technological and political changes of the twenty-first century have accentuated the degree of interdependence among nations and the importance of incorporating global awareness in the training of family science professionals. In order for family educators to function as professionals in a global society, colleges and universities have the responsibility to provide students and faculty with the opportunities to improve their knowledge and experience in this area. Direct exposure to other cultures seems to be the best way to learn about families in different cultural contexts. For example, the Fulbright programs under the Exchange of Scholars or the Educational Partnerships*, discussed in this chapter, show how involving faculty, students, and communities from different countries in common projects can enhance teaching and learning about international families. Experiencing first-hand variables such as values, reli-

---

*Readers interested in these and other exchange programs for U.S. scholars and those from other countries can visit the following Web sites: Council for the International Exchange of Scholars http://www.cies.org/; Fulbright Educational Partnerships Program http://exchanges.state.gov/education/partnership/fulbright.htm; U.S. Department of State Bureau of Education and Cultural Affairs (BECA) http://exchanges .state.gov/; Fulbright U.S. Scholar Program http://www.cies.org/us_scholars.

gion, community expectations, as well as the amount and nature of resources and their effects on the behavior of families and individuals can enhance global understanding. This understanding leads to the recognition of our commonalities and to the acceptance of differences that will certainly contribute to a better global community.

Family studies academic units should make information about the Fulbright and similar programs available to faculty and students. Additional support during the application process, as well as an environment that facilitates and encourages faculty involvement in these programs, are essential. Workshops and sessions sponsored by professional organizations and delivered by former awardees can increase the motivation of faculty to participate.

This chapter was limited to the author's experiences with two programs under the Fulbright umbrella. Further rigorous empirical analyses of data to determine the effect of these programs on the effectiveness of teaching and learning are needed in order to provide more specific recommendations.

APPENDIX: PARTICIPANTS' REPORT

A. Part I—Administrative
   1. Name
   2. Home address
   3. Host institution
   4. Field of specialization
   5. Period of visit
      a. Preparation for the exchange experience
      b. Transportation arrangements
      c. Financial arrangements: (Please comment on adequacy of stipend, supplies, etc.)
      d. Logistic arrangements abroad (please comment on availability and adequacy of the items described)
         i. Housing
         ii. Household furniture and furnishings
         iii. Food
         iv. Local transportation
         v. Medical and dental services
      e. Suggestions: Discuss freely any administrative matters you may wish to comment upon and add any recommendations.

B. Part II—Professional Activities: The following outline suggests the kind of information that would be useful for the evaluation of this exchange experience. However, you may organize your remarks in any way that you choose.
1. Description of your assignment
2. Do you feel that you were able to accomplish the objective of your assignment?
3. Please list and comment on the activities you were involved in during your visit. Did you develop or identify any materials that will be useful for your institution/community?
4. Could you comment on
   a. your professional relationship with faculty, staff, and administrators of the host institution
   b. your relationship with the community
5. Please recount occasions on which you addressed or spoke to local audiences, participated in cultural and professional meetings, etc.
6. Please evaluate your experience in terms of;
   a. professional value
   b. personal and social value
   c. contribution to international understanding
   d. the empowerment of women and consumers
7. Suggestions: Discuss freely any aspect of the grant, or the total experience, and offer any recommendation, which you believe, will enhance the program.
8. Any other comments?

REFERENCES

Anderson, C.L. (2003). Global interdependence: What does it really mean? *Journal of Family and Consumer Sciences, 95,* iii.

Andrews, M.P. (2000). The international dimension in AAHS? BOHS institutions: Status report, 1997. *Journal of Family and Consumer Sciences, 92,*109-110.

Andrews, M.P. (2003). Globalization: The role of FCS in shaping the new world community. *Journal of Family and Consumer Sciences, 95,* 4-8.

Bureau of Educational and Cultural Affairs (BECA) (2003). *Educational partnerships program.* Retrieved September 25, 2003, from http://exchanges.state.gov/education/partnership/fulbright.htm.

Council for International Exchange of Scholars (2004). Retrieved June 10, 2004, from mailto:cieswebmaster@cies.iie.org.

Crowford, G. (1993). Developing student global perspectives through undergraduate family resource management. *Journal of Home Economics, 85*(2), 9-15.

Firebaugh, F.M. & Deacon, R.E. (1990). International home economics programs in higher education. In S.K. Williams, D.L. Murray, & E.C. West (Eds.), *Looking toward the 21st century: Home economics and the global community* (pp. 215-227). Mission Hills, CA: Glencoe/McGraw Hill.

Firebaugh, F.M. & Miller, J.R. (2000). Diversity and globalization: Challenges, opportunities, and promise. *Journal of Family and Consumer Sciences, 92,* 27-36.

Gomes, P. & Mallonee, M. (2002). *Impact of the U.S. Fulbright Scholar program evaluated by SRI International.* Retrieved September 25, 2003, from http://www.cies.org/Press_Release/PR_SRIstudy.htm.

Hanvey, R.G. (1979). *Possibilities for international/global education: A report.* New York: Global Perspectives in Education.

Harari, M. (1981). *Internationalizing the curriculum and the campus: Guidelines for AASCU institutions.* Washington, DC: American Association of State College and Universities (AASCU).

Institute for International Education (2004). *Fulbright program overview.* Retrieved June 10, 2004, from http://www.iie.org/FulbrightTemplate.cfm?Section= Fulbright_Program_Overview.

Kameoka, Y. (1996). The internationalization of higher education. *The OECD Observer, 204,* 34-36.

Paige, R.C. & Williams, S.K. (2001). Perceptions of university seniors toward internationalizing curriculum in family and consumer sciences: Have we made progress? *Journal of Family and Consumer Sciences, 93,* 79-83.

Tucker, K.S. (2003). Having a global view is now a basic life skill. *Journal of Family and Consumer Sciences, 95,* 3.

Chapter 8

Teaching Family Science in Ecuador

Paul L. Schvaneveldt
Bron B. Ingoldsby

Even though colleges and universities in the United States and other Western industrialized countries have been offering courses in family relations since the 1930s, discussions of a coherent discipline of family science did not really emerge until the 1980s (NCFR Task Force, 1988). Since that time, there has been considerable attention paid to the many programs that offer professional training in this area (Day, Quick, Leigh, & McKenry, 1988) and the various career options that exist for graduates in the field (Holman & Vance, 1989).

The teaching of a family science curriculum to undergraduates in colleges or universities in the countries of Latin America is extremely rare. A tradition of training for family therapy in a few countries exists, such as Argentina, but the teaching of the principles of child development, parenting, and marriage appears to have little appeal as part of undergraduate education. These issues fall into the category of everyday, normal living and not career preparation. Although Latino families are studied with increasing frequency in the United States (Bean, Crane & Lewis, 2002), and are a focus for policy and program efforts (Zambrana, 1995), there is little scholarship in Latin American countries about its own family life.

The following account illustrates this mind-set. A colleague was recently visiting a university in Cuenca, Ecuador, where he learned of the development of a graduate-level family therapy program. He asked about coursework in general family science, and the faculty seemed surprised at the notion. The response to his question by the

doi:10.1300/5609_08

139

developers of the new program was one of bewilderment. The program developers did not understand that the general public needs training for marriage or parenting, and saw little value of such courses in the academic world. The program developers also had drawn little on the North American literature and expertise for developing their family therapy program, being relatively unaware of it. As they had already dedicated too much time and effort into an almost completed curriculum, the North American colleague was asked *not* to provide them with these additional resources.

Years of research and service experience in Latin America convinced the authors that the described approach is "typical." More traditional disciplines such as sociology are common, but family science or human ecology is virtually nonexistent. We have recently become aware of an exception, which may portend the growth of the family discipline into the countries of Latin America. Much of the information comes from on-site visits, interviews with program directors, brochures, and the Web site of the University of Casa Grande (2004; www.casagrande.edu.ec). (Access was gained due to a working relationship with Dr. Uribe who is the dean in the School of Communication at Casa Grande University) (see Ingoldsby, Schvaneveldt & Uribe 2003).

The authors have gained much experience in Latin America through involvement over the past twenty years in Partners of the Americas (www.partners.net). Partners is an nongovernmental organization (NGO) developed in the Kennedy Administration at the same time as the Peace Corps. Each state is connected with a country in Latin America for development and service projects. Scholars from many disciplines are often involved. Through Partners and similar activities, we have developed connections with other professionals who work with families in Ecuador and other Andean countries.

CASE EXAMPLE: CASA GRANDE

After twenty-one years in Chile and nine years in Ecuador, the Monica Herrera School of Communication became the University of Casa Grande (or Big House). This private university was certified by the Ecuadorian National Congress in May 1999. It is located in Guayaquil, Ecuador's largest and principal port city. It has a population of about two million.

According to its public relations materials (i.e., pamphlets), the university boasts an innovative and demanding curriculum, based on successful models from other nations such as Chile and Argentina. Academic professionals from outside the country join with the local faculty in providing flexible programs to meet the needs of students (Universidad Casa Grande, 2004). Students are required to have a command of English, as many classes and textbooks are published in what has become the international language of business and education. Most students are from privileged backgrounds and Casa Grande is viewed as one of the more elite universities in Ecuador (M. Carmingniani, personal interview, August 2003). Foreign students from the United States or elsewhere are welcome to apply and would learn a great deal about family science within the context of Latino families if they did.

The campus consists of a series of contiguous buildings which were originally private residences. Even though it is near downtown Guayaquil, the setting is closed off, attractive, and tranquil. The university consists of three schools: Communication; Administration and Political Science; and Human Ecology, Education, and Development. Casa Grande operates on a semester system of two 4.5-month terms (April to August, and August to December) and one more intensive three-month term during January to March (Universidad Casa Grande, 2004).

The program in human ecology was started at Casa Grande University because the president completed graduate studies in Paris, where she learned of Bronfenbrenner's (1979; 1986) theory of ecological development. The president then established the College of Human Ecology based on those experiences. Dr. Jay Rivera, a U.S. national and developmental psychologist who studied at American University in the United States, developed the program in the 1990s. Because Dr. Rivera's specialty is in educational psychology, the program emphasized human development over family studies, but the family counseling courses do focus on internal family dynamics. No other university in Latin America has developed a human ecology or family studies program.

HUMAN ECOLOGY

Human ecology is the first program of its kind in Ecuador and, as claimed in the Casa Grande brochures, the first and only human ecology program in South America (Facultad de Ecología Humana, Educación, y Desarrollo, 2003). The program's goal is to train graduate professionals to understand the interaction of human beings within their social environment, and be capable of intervening in ways which facilitate social and personal development within the various contexts of their lives. Graduates will be social scientists in the same category as psychologists, sociologists, and educators. They may work in the private or public sectors, with international organizations or in self-owned, private practice.

Four-year bachelor's or technical degrees in human ecology are offered with specialization in infant and child development, family counseling, international education, and management of community programs. Descriptions of the principal options are discussed as follows (Facultad de Ecologìa Humana, Educaciòn, y Desarrollo, 2003).

Infant and Child Development

Students who want to be involved with the teaching of children in general or with those who have learning problems or handicaps should choose this course. You will learn to plan and administer programs for children and their families, as well as stimulation programs for infants.

Family Counseling

Students who like the idea of being a family counselor and enjoy working with people, will find this program a good option. In this program students learn to counsel families in crisis, help people deal with their addictions, enhance their marital relations, or improve parent-child problems.

International Education

Students in the international education program learn how to teach foreign language and about different cultures that speak Spanish and English. This course provides a multilingual, multicultural, and broad perspective on other countries. English teachers, early childhood teachers, or others who wish to advance their professional development and receive a new degree, will find this program helpful.

Management of Community Programs

In the management of community programs major, students will obtain a two-year technical certificate. Students receive a general orientation for the administration of development organizations, more specifically, nongovernmental organizations (NGO's) that are multidisciplinary in focus. The program offers a four-year degree for those who are looking to become creative leaders with the capacity to develop new models of human development that respond to the complex challenges of a new millennium in a systematic, multidisciplinary, and ethical manner.

Possible employment opportunities for graduates include teaching in elementary and secondary schools as well as university-level teaching. Other areas of employment include hospitals, special education centers, educational support centers, private and public social development organizations, nongovernmental organizations, and private companies.

THE CURRICULUM

The first two years of the program consist of the basic courses of human ecology; in the third and fourth years students select a focus option (i.e., infant and child development, family counseling, etc.). The fourth year is dedicated to practical skills development, practicum experiences, case studies, and a senior capstone project. A total of 145 credit hours are required for the degree, and tuition presently costs $1,000 per semester. The entire curriculum is presented in Exhibit 8.1.

The following information is based on a face-to-face interview with Dean Gilda Macias Carmingniani, Human Ecology, conducted in August of 2003. Most of the students in human ecology at Casa Grande have a goal of opening a private practice to treat other middle/upper socioeconomic status (SES) children and families or to teach children in private schools. SES reflects one's education level and income. Typically, persons with higher levels of education (four-year university degree or higher) and a higher income are considered to be middle/upper SES background, whereas those with a high-school-level education or lower and corresponding lower levels of income are considered to be from a lower SES background. Students at Casa Grande University mostly come from middle/upper SES backgrounds. Many do go on to achieve these goals, but others find that there are already psychologists and teachers providing services to these clients, and therefore must look at other options for employment, such as working with lower SES populations, or for the Ecuadorian

EXHIBIT 8.1. Human Ecology Required courses

First-year courses for all Human Ecology students

General Pedagogy	Psychology I	Communication I
Biology of Development	Research Methods I	Rhetoric
Use of Audiovisuals in Teaching	Use of Games and Activities in Teaching	Nutrition
Case Study I	Theories of Learning	Psychology II
Writing of Reports	Neuropsychology	Research Methods II
Technical Problem Solving	Critical Thought	Creative Thought
Field Experience I		

Second-year courses for all Human Ecology students

Human Development	Curriculum Planning	Resilience and Human Development
Organizational Communication	Health Education	Project Design
Quantitative Statistics	Community Program Management	Business Management
Case Study II	Social Psychology	Anthropology I
Developmental Models	Process of Change	Introduction to Areas of Specialization
Evaluation of Projects	Counseling	Field Experience II

Third-year courses for all Human Ecology students

Anthropology II	Sociology I	Family Theory
Oral and Written Communication (English)	Case Study III	Cultural Investigation
Contemporary Social Problems	Field Experience III	

Fourth-year courses for all Human Ecology students

Modernity and Postmodernity of Social Institutions	Professional Ethics	Case Study IV
Field Experience IV	Seminar on Licensing	

Third-year courses Infant and Child Development majors

Study of Disabilities	Art and Play Education	Evaluation of Children ages 0-3

Design and Materials of Early Stimulation	Design of Learning Environments	Theory of Early Stimulation
Beginning Curriculum Planning		

Fourth-year courses Infant and Child Development majors

Development and Evaluation of Children 3-6	Psychological Evaluation of Children	Design and Materials for Children 3-6
Context and Disabilities	Intervention with Children at Risk	Personal Development
Protective Systems for Children and Families	School Administration	Psychometrics
Math for Children	Curriculum Planning for Inclusion	

Third-year courses for Family Counseling

Context and Family Models	Contemporary Family Problems	Evaluation and Diagnosis of Families I
Family Counseling I	Qualitative Research Methods	Field Experience III
Evaluation and Diagnosis of Families II	Psychopathology	

Fourth-year courses for Family Counseling

Brief Psychotherapies	Protective Systems for Children and Families	Personal Development
Family and Gender	Introduction to Psychoanalysis	Psychotherapy Experience I
Disability in Context	Society and Economics	Methods of Intervention for Children at Risk
Sexuality and the Family	Family Counseling II	Legal Issues and the Family
Psychotherapy Experience II		

Third-year courses for Management of Community Programs

Economy and Society	Outcomes Evaluations	Social and Political Development
Research Methods I	Psychology I	Marking of Services
Negotiation	Communication II	Introduction to Sociopolitical Analysis
Contemporary Views on Human Resources	Management of Public Politics in Ecuador	Research Methods II

(continued)

(continued)

Fourth-year courses for Management of Community Programs

Systematic Social Experiences	Development of Networks	International Politics
Political Economy of Ecuador	Selection and Hiring of Personnel	Gender and the Family
Negotiation II	Quantitative Research Methods	Social Psychology
Management and Control of Community Programs	Management and Production of Services	Diversity and Development
Decentralized Public Management		

government. Most of the students in the infant and child development major find work during their third and fourth years as child care providers and easily find full-time employment at formal child care centers upon graduation. In fact, the offering of courses was changed to accommodate work schedules to allow students to work at child care facilities in the morning and attend classes in the afternoon.

Family Counseling Program

Students in the family counseling program are taught how to plan and implement an intervention for a family. They are given a case study and then develop the treatment and intervention program for that specific family context. The students also gain practical experience with the field study that they must complete annually. They are required to visit lower SES barrios or neighborhoods to do field interviews and determine the needs of a family. The assignment then is to prepare a plan of action and intervention.

Examples of interventions include parenting counseling, grief counseling, couple communication, or domestic violence prevention or intervention. Target populations in the past have been persons with AIDS, crime victims, persons in poverty, and/or recent immigrant farmers from rural areas. A major goal of this field experience is to expose students to diverse populations and experiences. Because most of the students come from middle/upper SES backgrounds, most have had very little contact with persons who have serious economic and other challenges.

Management of Community Program

The management of community programs major is focused on developing social capital in Latin America. A major goal is to develop networks and programs to bring about political activism and systemic changes in the broader society. Most of the students are older, with work experience, and are already working in human services in some capacity. They are motivated to become more informed on how to manage social services.

Students in all majors are required to complete a senior capstone project, which is similar to a master's thesis project in the United States. Students develop a proposal, which is reviewed by a faculty committee, and then gather information and implement their project, the results of which are finally presented to the committee. Upon successful completion of revisions suggested by the faculty committee members, students are recommended for graduation.

Casa Grande recognizes that its human ecology program may serve as a model for other institutions. The faculty have a great commitment to their students and to the institutions which may implement this new (in Latin America) profession into their curricula in the future. Note that these degrees are offered at the undergraduate level, rather than as a master's degree, as would be typical in the United States.

Presently, it is administered by Dr. Gilda Macìas Carmigniani, dean of the College of Human Ecology, and an Ecuadorian national. Other faculty members include Dr. Mariana Chadwick, a psychology professor from Chile, and Martha Beato, a psychotherapist from the Dominican Republic who specializes in transactional analysis. In spite of the fact that all of the leaders in the program are psychologists, they have a very cross-disciplinary definition of Human Ecology. They see it is as a social science, drawing from psychology, anthropology, sociology, philosophy, history, economics, teaching, communication, administration, the fine arts, mathematics, ecology, and political science.

DISCUSSION

These family science programs are still in a process of revision and change. The School of Human Ecology originally offered a degree in human resource management that has since been dropped, and a new major in special education will soon be offered. Much of the curriculum has changed since it began just a few years ago, and we expect it to continue to evolve. Currently, students with a four-year bachelor's degree are qualified to become family therapists. The faculty feel that the students lack the life experience and maturity to deal with serious family issues.

During the site visit with the dean, she was informed of the National Council on Family Relations Ten Content Areas for Family Life Education (Buck, Campbell, Chatelain, Higginson, & Merrill, 1999). Curricula will be altered to prepare undergraduate students in these areas of family life education, and family therapy will become a graduate program as is commonly done in the United States.

As one can see from the list of classes in Exhibit 8.1, this program is in its infancy, and does not yet meet the standards of the field in the United States (Powell & Cassidy, 2001). However, even though many of the content courses that one might expect in a family curriculum are still missing, Casa Grande does emphasize the skills training approach that has been recommended by some professionals (Brock, 1987).

Interestingly, students in the family therapy program undergo personal therapy as they are learning the therapeutic approach. Also, students are required to work on case studies and field experiences each semester. The purpose is to provide students with applied experience in working with children and families. The students are given a case study of a family that describes a family issue such as family violence, chronic unemployment, substance abuse, or other serious family issues. The students then design a treatment or intervention strategy based upon the case study. In the field experience, students go into low-income neighborhoods and work with children and families. Since most students come from privileged backgrounds, they are unaware of the dire conditions of the poor in Ecuador. Many students are shocked and horrified at the abject poverty, family violence, and other social problems they encounter. The field experience is designed to promote an awareness of the difficult circumstances many families face in Ecuador.

The future of the family science program is somewhat unclear. In its short history, it has seen three deans and many changes to the curriculum. However, most students find work in their fields of study, which leads us to believe the program will endure. Because this is the only human ecology program in Ecuador, most students find they are uniquely qualified for employment in an area in which demand could not be met previously. The faculty will continue to make alterations as their knowledge increases and resources fluctuate.

To date, very little research and study has focused on the many Latino subgroups in the United States, much less in the countries of origin. In fact, some claim that family sociology has masked, rather than clarified important differences in its investigations of Latino family life (Baca Zinn & Wells, 2000). Family science programs in the local universities of the various countries in Latin America could go a long way toward rectifying this problem while training their own people in family life education and therapy. Clearly, there is a need for formal education in family issues in Latin America, and our hope is that the Casa Grande program will serve as a catalyst for the development of other programs in the region.

REFERENCES

Baca Zinn, M. & Wells, B. (2000). Diversity within Latino families: New lessons for family social science. In D. Demo, K. Allen, & M. Fine, (Eds.). *Handbook of Family Diversity* (pp. 252-273). New York: Oxford University Press.

Bean, R., Crane, R., & Lewis, T. (2002). Basic research and implications for practice in family science: A content analysis and status report for U.S. ethnic groups. *Family Relations, 51,* 15-21.

Brock, G. (1987). Family science undergraduate programs: It's time for a new approach. *Family Science Review, 1(1),* 74-78.

Bronfenbrenner, U. (1979). *The ecology of human development.* Cambridge, MA: Harvard University Press.

Bronfenbrenner, U. (1986). Ecology of the family as context for human development: Research perspectives. *Developmental Psychology, 22,* 723-742.

Buck, J., Campbell, C., Chatelain, R., Higginson, R., & Merrill, C. (1999). *Competencies for family life educators.* Minneapolis, MN: National Council on Family Relations.

Day, R., Quick, D., Leigh, G., & McKenry, P. (1988). Professional training in family science: A review of undergraduate and graduate programs. *Family Science Review, 1(4),* 313-348.

Facultad de Ecologìa Humana, Educaciòn, y Desarrollo (Faculty of Human Ecology, Education, and Development; 2003). Informational brochure. Guayaquil, Ecuador: Universidad Casa Grande.

Holman, T. & Vance, B. (Eds.) (1989). Special issue on career and professional development in family science. *Family Science Review, 2(1).*

Ingoldsby, B., Schvaneveldt, P., & Uribe, C. (2003). Perceptions of acceptable mate attributes in Ecuador. *Journal of Comparative Family Studies, 34,* 171-185.

NCFR Task Force on the development of a family discipline (1988). What is family science? *Family Science Review, 1(2),* 87-101.

Powell, L. & Cassidy, D. (2001). *Family life education: An introduction.* Mt. View, CA: Mayfield.

Universidad Casa Grande (2004). Information retrieved on January 23, 2004, from http://www.casagrande.edu.ec.

Zambrana, R. (1995). *Understanding Latino families: Scholarship, policy and practice.* Thousand Oaks, CA: Sage.

PART II: TEACHING TOOLS AND TECHNIQUES

Chapter 9

Teaching About Ethnic Families Using Student Group Presentations

Sylvia Niehuis

PURPOSE, OBJECTIVES, AND RATIONALE

Purpose

- Enhance students' knowledge about families of different ethnic backgrounds
- Help students develop oral presentation and teamwork skills

Objectives

Implementation of this teaching strategy should:

I would like to thank Daren Olson, Adam Munk, Julie Roope, and Reva Rosenband, who have helped me to develop and refine the idea of student group presentations. My thanks also go to Paul Miller and Denise Bartell for their helpful comments on earlier versions of this chapter.

doi:10.1300/5609_09

151

- Increase students' knowledge about an assigned ethnic group
- Raise students' awareness of interpersonal barriers that stand in the way of effective interaction with people from different cultural backgrounds
- Improve students' ability to work in teams and present information orally

Rationale

Many students in family science classes want to learn about people from different ethnic backgrounds. They realize that it is important in today's world to know more about diversity and to be competent in dealing with people from diverse origins. At the same time, they often feel intimidated about interacting with people from diverse ethnic backgrounds for fear of not understanding them and accidentally offending them. Students also often lack the skills to work with individuals and families outside the academic setting, especially if these individuals and families come from different ethnic experiences.

Cultural diversity often presents a problem in organizations that deal with individuals and families as well. A clear discrepancy exists between the skills new hires possess and the level of skills organizations desire new hires to have (American Management Association, 1997). New employees are particularly deficient in terms of their ability to relate to others, their oral communication skills, and their teamwork skills (Bucher, 2004). Thus, instructors of family science classes need to ask themselves (1) How can they help students overcome their fears, acquire knowledge about families of different ethnic backgrounds, and become competent in interaction with ethnically diverse families?; and (2) How can they teach students skills required by employers today, such as the ability to communicate orally, to take the initiative, to relate to others, and to work effectively in a team?

With these questions in mind, I have organized my upper division undergraduate class (80-100 students) on family and cultural diversity (with particular focus on ethnic diversity in the United States) in such a way as to help students to both become knowledgeable about families of different ethnic backgrounds and also develop oral and teamwork skills. Approximately 50 percent of the class periods per semester are taught by me, the other 50 percent by the students in my class. The class periods held by the students cover information on twenty different types of ethnic families in the United States, selected to represent

- ethnic families from different parts of the world (e.g., European ethnic minorities, Hispanic ethnic minorities, Asian ethnic minorities, African ethnic minorities);
- subgroups of larger ethnic groups (e.g., Japanese Americans, Chinese Americans, Vietnamese Americans, etc., rather than just Asian Americans);
- historically subjugated ethnic groups (e.g., African Americans and Native Americans);
- socioreligious ethnic minorities (e.g., Jewish Americans, the Amish, and the Mormons); and
- recent immigrant groups (e.g., Russian Americans and Nigerian Americans).

Each type of ethnic family is covered by one student group during one class period. Student groups are asked to actively explore an assigned ethnic group, using some readings I make available to them, as well as other sources. Their task is to examine the assigned ethnic group's family relationships in the country of origin; the historical, economic, and political factors that lead to immigration to the United States; any barriers that may have been encountered in the United States; changes in the family relationships since immigration to the United States; and demographic trends and social problems this ethnic group may experience. Students are also encouraged to explore these topics through direct contact with a member of their assigned ethnic group or a professional working with members of this ethnic group. Student groups are allowed to either invite a guest speaker to class or to show a videotaped interview in class, provided that this part of the presentation does not last more than ten minutes.

The student group presentation technique differs from conventional student presentations, in that each student group presentation takes up almost the entire class period (forty minutes out of a fifty-minute class session). It involves extensive research and oral communication practice on the part of the students, and intensive mentoring on the part of the instructor. The technique can be used in any type of upper division class that (1) does not exceed 100 students, and (2) deals with topics that are distinctly different from one another and can be covered in single class periods. In my experience, groups of three to four students are most effective.

A plethora of research demonstrates the effectiveness of team-work and peer teaching over more traditional, and typically instruc-tor-centered, teaching methods (e.g., Barr & Tagg, 1995; Feldman & Newcomb, 1969; Klippert, 1998; McKeachie, 1999; Svinicki, 1991). Teamwork allows students to:

1. gather and process information (e.g., studying facts, under-standing phenomena, evaluating information, observing pat-terns, excerpting information, and organizing facts);
2. practice social-communicative skills (e.g., listening to others in the group, providing arguments, asking questions, cooperating on smaller tasks, integrating information from several group members, and presenting information to others); and
3. engage in affective learning (e.g., developing self-esteem, tak-ing initiative, learning about one's own abilities, aptitudes, and skills) (Klippert, 1998).

Preparing a class presentation and subsequently teaching the mate-rial to peers requires active thinking about the material, making delib-erate choices about the selection of the material to be presented, mak-ing decisions about how to present the information most effectively, and understanding and conceptualizing the material in one's own words (Bargh & Schul 1980; Barr & Tagg, 1995; Feldman & New-comb, 1969; McKeachie, 1999; Singelis, 1998; Svinicki, 1991).

Compared to instructor-centered teaching, student group presenta-tions are particularly effective in teaching knowledge about different ethnic families in the United States because students actively explore and learn about an ethnic group and then present this information to their classmates. Students are able to experience cultural perspectives by visiting with and interviewing members of their assigned ethnic groups. For example, students may try to make contact with members of their assigned ethnic group by visiting religious services, attending ethnic festivals, arranging a meeting with members of the different ethnic student clubs on campus, etc. They are encouraged to inter-view the people they meet about the following issues.

1. Life, family relationship patterns, values, etc., in their country of origin and their subsequent immigration experience (e.g., How were boys and girls socialized in the country of origin? What were reasons for leaving the country of origin? What was the immigration experience like?).
2. The impact of the immigration experience on their family (e.g., How did the family deal with increased levels of stress? How did the roles of the different family members change as a result of coming to the United States?).
3. Barriers that may have stood in the way of effective intercultural relationships (e.g., Did the interviewee experience language difficulties and how much did that affect his or her day-to-day life? Did the interviewee experience prejudice, discrimination, or ethnocentrism, and how did this influence interaction with others?).

This personal contact is important because it helps students to understand some of the barriers that may have prevented or made difficult effective intercultural relations. It also increases students' awareness of some of the barriers that may make them reluctant to interact with their interviewee. Often, students begin to learn that if they are patient and make an effort, they eventually overcome some of their own reservations about interacting with others. This makes them open to future interactions with people from different ethnic backgrounds. Furthermore, personal contact with a member of a different ethnic group helps students recognize that the attitudes and behaviors of their interviewee may differ from the cultural norms they have studied for their presentation. That is, students learn that although it is important to have knowledge about different ethnic groups, it is equally important to understand that one cannot make generalized assumptions about people based on their cultural affiliation.

Finally, active (rather than passive) interaction with the course materials makes it more meaningful for students, increases their interest in the class material, and enhances their professional and interpersonal skills. One of the biggest lessons students learn is that they are more similar to others than they are different. This realization is necessary to decrease fears, to increase empathy, and to make effective interpersonal relations possible.

PROCEDURE

First Day of Class

Before the semester starts, I obtain a list of all students in the class and randomly place them in groups of three to four students. Each group is then assigned an ethnic family type to study. I assign students to a group randomly rather than allowing students to choose their own group because I want to ensure that the groups will be heterogeneous in terms of students' abilities, attitudes, and behaviors. Moreover, I want to avoid situations in which students who know each other might collaborate more closely with one another, while students unknown to the other group members might be left out.

Each person in a student group receives the names and e-mail addresses of his or her fellow group members, and a list of references for chapters and articles on the assigned ethnic group that can be used for the group presentation. I request that at least two of the sources listed be used for the presentation. Because some of the references are hard to obtain, I make all of them available to students on electronic and regular reserve. Students are encouraged to go beyond those readings to become more knowledgeable and to make their presentation more interesting.

On the first day of class I introduce students to the idea of student group presentations, explaining both the assignment and my reasons for using presentations in class. I tell students that they can research their assigned ethnic group using academic articles, chapters, information from the Internet, newspapers, and other resources to examine the following topics:

- family relationships in the country of origin (e.g., gender roles in the family, family structure, family values and strengths, and intergenerational relationships in the family)
- historical, economic, and political factors that lead to immigration to the United States
- barriers encountered in the United States (e.g., discrimination, prejudice, and immigration laws)
- family relationships in the United States (e.g., acculturation processes, family roles and responsibilities, values and attitudes, family life-cycle patterns, and kinship ties)

- demographic trends and social problems (e.g., fertility, age at marriage, marital disruption, household size and composition, education, employment, poverty, social class, health, language skills, and ethnic intermarriage)
- healing beliefs and practices (e.g., attitudes, beliefs, and practices regarding health, health practices, and practitioners)
- religious/spiritual beliefs and practices

I also inform students that they are expected to present their research findings in a forty-minute class presentation. Each participant in the group is expected to speak during the group presentation. To help them stay within the time limit, students are encouraged to time themselves while practicing the presentation. The information is to be presented in an engaging style that will actively involve the class members in the learning process (e.g., by leading a discussion or organizing mini-activities). For ideas that may be adapted for their presentations, I refer students to Silberman's (1996) book on teaching strategies designed to engage the audience in active learning, which is available to them on reserve.

Students also learn that they are required to prepare a presentation outline that will assist their classmates in taking notes on the content of the student group presentation. The goal of the outline is to help their classmates to take notes—not to take the notes for them. Having student groups develop an outline of their presentation helps them to organize their presentation and to make conscious decisions about the important information they wish their classmates to learn. Moreover, the student audience profits from the outline because note taking is an activity which (1) helps them to stay attentive, (2) allows them to process information at a deeper level, and (3) aids them in learning and recalling the information (Kiewra, 1989; McKeachie, 1999; Peper & Mayer, 1978; Weiland & Kingsbury, 1979). It is the student groups' responsibility to make copies of the handout available to all students in class on the day the presentation is due.

Finally, I explain to students how the student group presentations will be evaluated. I go over the individual criteria that both I and my teaching assistant use to evaluate the presentation, and I also make students aware of their role in evaluating their group members' performance. The students' evaluations of one another and my teaching assistant's and my own evaluation of the presentation determine students' final grades on the presentation. All the information about the assignment, including the grading criteria I use to evaluate students and the form students need to fill out to evaluate their group members' performance, are made available to the students in a handout.

In addition to explaining the assignment to students, I also share with the students my reasons for using student group presentations in my class. These reasons are the same as those presented in the rationale section presented previously. I conclude the first day of class by urging students to obtain the references recommended for their assigned ethnic group and to have them read by the time of the organizational meeting held during the second week of class.

Second Week of Class

To help students get started, one class period during the second week of class is devoted to getting organized. For this class session, I prepare copies of a weekly planner that students can use to figure out when they have time to meet with one another. Students also use this class period to exchange contact information, e.g., phone and e-mail. Finally, students use the time to decide how to split up the broader areas within their assigned topic. Having students read the recommended literature in advance helps them to get an idea of which topics to research and how to split up the work among the group members.

Throughout the Semester

The Instructor-Student Meetings

Over the course of the semester I schedule two meetings with each student group. Both meetings last thirty to sixty minutes each. The first of these meetings takes place at least two weeks prior to the class presentation (but preferably as early in the semester as possible). All members of a student group are required to meet with me to discuss the content of their presentation, to show me their outline for their classmates, and to inform me about planned discussion questions or activities. Students are expected to come to the first meeting with: a detailed outline of the information they intend to cover in their presentation, the sources they have used for their presentation, a clear conception of who will present what information, and specific ideas of how they intend to present this information. This gives me the opportunity to make sure the information is appropriate and covers important content. During this meeting, I also ask students to explain to me how they intend to deliver the information and how they will prepare their talk. I use this time to discuss practical concerns with presentations (e.g., making sure the font they use on their PowerPoint presentation will be large enough so students in the back can read everything), strategies for preparing and carrying out the oral part of the presentation (e.g., practicing the speech at home and maintaining eye contact with the audience for the duration of the presentation), and the use of activities or discussions that will actively involve the audience in the learning process. Talking about activities and discussion is important, because many students seem to think that games or video clips are the only creative way of teaching the material and that discussions are easy to carry out and do not require considerable preparation. If students cannot think of activities to use for their presentation, I remind them to consult Silberman's (1996) book and to meet with me again to discuss an activity they think can be adapted for their presentation. Finally, I reemphasize the enormous responsibility student presenters have toward the rest of their classmates. I make it absolutely clear that I have high expectations of them and that I grade accordingly. At the same time, I try to assure students that they are not expected to be the experts on the topic and that it is okay to admit to their classmates or me if they do not know the answer to a question.

The second meeting occurs approximately one week prior to the class presentation and takes place in the classroom where students will give their talk. Having this second meeting helps me to show students how to operate the various equipment they will need for their presentation and to see whether students have made the necessary changes to their presentation since our first meeting. It also helps the students to practice their presentation and to become aware of any issues related to the quality of the presentation. Typically, I sit in the back of the room while students give the presentation. As I watch their presentation, I pay particular attention to (1) the quality of the presentation itself (i.e., the quality of the PowerPoint presentation, the presenters' oral skills, etc.); and (2) the content of the presentation (i.e., is the information correct, complete, easy to understand?). I have the grading criteria for the presentation with me and typically share my feedback after each presentation segment.

The Presentation

The presentations begin during the fourth week of class. On the day of the student presentation, I arrive approximately fifteen minutes before class starts to assist in setting up the necessary equipment (e.g., computer, projector, video recorder, and microphone). I also collect a copy of the outline students have prepared for their classmates. Once it is time to begin, I introduce the entire class to the topic of the student group. Then the presentation begins. At the end of the presentation, I point out the most important or distinguishing facts about the particular ethnic group that were presented and, if necessary, add any important information that the group may have omitted. I also compare and contrast the ethnic group that was presented with another ethnic group. For example, I compare (or ask students to compare) the present ethnic group with a previously presented ethnic group in terms of their similarities or differences in regard to some aspect(s) of culture.

The Evaluation of the Presentation

Both my teaching assistant and I observe the presentation and grade it according to the following grading criteria:

1. *Content of the presentation*
   How well was important information covered?
   Were assertions valid and supported?
   How well did students explain how the information presented was applicable to their peers' personal or future professional life?
   Did students inform their classmates about the sources of their information?
2. *Quality of the presentation*
   Was the presentation engaging?
   How well were class activities and discussions planned and carried out?
   How well was the presentation organized?

Were the materials presented in class easy to read?
Could the presenters be heard in the back?
Did the presenters make eye contact with the audience?
3. *Quality of the presentation outline*
Does the content of the handout follow the organization of the presentation?
Is there enough space between each heading for students to take notes?

Each of these criteria is weighted equally, and points are taken off when students fail to meet the criteria. Once the class session is over, I ask each member of the student group to turn in the form on which they evaluated the members of their group on their overall contribution to the presentation. A student's final grade is the average of my own, my teaching assistant's, and the group members' average peer evaluation of the student. This grading system has been adopted because neither my teaching assistant nor I can possibly know the quality and quantity that each individual student contributes to the class presentation; thus, we only evaluate the quality of the actual presentation. The members of the student group, however, are in a position to evaluate one another's contribution to the presentation, and thus, their mutual evaluations are figured into the overall grade for each person. As a result, group members will often receive different grades for the presentation. Students having to work in teams often worry about freeloaders (i.e., other students who do not do their fair share of the work and still receive credit). The grading method employed in this assignment ensures that freeloaders will receive lower grades for their lack of contribution to the presentation.

THE TEACHING STRATEGY'S EFFECTIVENESS

Anecdotal evidence suggests that both student presenters and student audiences respond very positively to this teaching strategy. In their class evaluations, student teachers have frequently reported that they have initially dreaded the idea of having to present in front of a large class. However, most of them report in their evaluations that they have enjoyed the assignment a great deal. Specifically, they have enjoyed being able to learn information on their assigned ethnic group in an active, independent way, rather than passively absorbing information delivered by somebody else. They have enjoyed sharing what they have learned with other students and creatively presenting the information to their peers. For example, some students have used role-play to teach about issues that lead to conflict between different generations of immigrant families. Others have given their presentation in the style of a news broadcast, having anchors in the "studio" (i.e., presenters in the classroom) to present facts and reporters "on location" (i.e., showing videotaped interviews of members of their assigned ethnic group). Still others have used small discussion groups to debate controversial issues (e.g., how people feel about illegal immigrants) or mind-mapping to prime students for the content of the presentation. Mind mapping is a graphic technique involving several cortical skills, such as word, image, number, logic, rhythm, color, and spatial awareness to create mental associations and improve learning.

Student group presentations have motivated many of the students to study other class topics on their own as well. Students have also shared with me that they like to take turns listening to others' presentations. Most students see the presentations as "fun," "interesting," and "exciting." As a result, many students feel that "it helps . . . learn the material better" and that the information "just sticks better." From comments students write in their class evaluations and other assignments, it has become apparent that their attitudes about people from different ethnic backgrounds have changed as a result of gaining knowledge from student presentations. For example, one student wrote, "Immigrants have to go through a lot to get here and through this experience I gained a greater respect for them." Moreover, students have also transferred information they learned from student group presentations to other assignments. For example, I require students to interview either a professional working with a culturally diverse population or a recent immigrant about their experiences. One student wrote in her interview paper: "It does help that I have a better understanding about some different cultures because of the presentations in class. I was able to keep those people in mind while going through this interview . . . There is so much that I have learned from this assignment." For one student, gaining knowledge about different ethnic families has had a positive effect on how she carries out her job: "This . . . has even affected the way I do my job. In retail sales, I help a lot of Mexican Americans and I would often become frustrated when I couldn't communicate with them. But now I try to make things easier for *them*—not me."

Students' learning of the information covered in the student group presentations is assessed in exams. A comparison of the average grades on exams before and since the implementation of student group presentations suggests that students profit from this teaching strategy. Although the overall content covered in my class has remained the same, students' grades on exams have improved. For example, before I used student group presentations, the average grade on an exam was 79 percent; since I have started using the student group presentations, the average grade on an exam is 84 percent. Obviously, making these comparisons is not ideal, since the exam questions (though very similar in content) change from semester to semester; moreover, other confounding factors, such as cohort effects, time of day the class is being held, etc., may affect grades as well. Nonetheless, these comparisons provide an (albeit imperfect) idea of the effectiveness of this teaching strategy in terms of student learning.

CONCLUSION

Using student group presentations effectively teaches students about various ethnic families and increases their awareness of barriers to successful intercultural relationships. Moreover, they help students gain valuable experience in working in teams and presenting information orally to their classmates.

REFERENCES

American Management Association (October, 1997). *What do organizations really want?* AMA Catalog of Seminars.

Bargh, J. A. & Schul, Y. (1980). On the cognitive benefits of teaching. *Journal of Educational Psychology, 72,* 593-604.

Barr, R. B. & Tagg, J. (1995). From teaching to learning—A new paradigm for undergraduate education. *Change, 27,* 12-25.

Bucher, R. D. (2004). *Diversity consciousness: Opening our minds to people, cultures, and opportunities* (Second edition). Upper Saddle River, NJ: Prentice-Hall.

Feldman, K. A. & Newcomb, T. M. (1969). *The impact of college on students* (Vol. 2). San Francisco: Jossey-Bass.

Kiewra, K. A. (1989). A review of note taking: The encoding storage paradigm and beyond. *Educational Psychology Review, 1,* 147-172.

Klippert, H. (1998). *Teamentwicklung im Klassenraum.* Weinheim, Germany: Beltz Verlag.

McKeachie, W. J. (1999). *McKeachie's teaching tips: Strategies, research, and theory for college and university teachers* (Tenth edition). Boston: Houghton Mifflin.

Peper, R. J. & Mayer, R. E. (1978). Note taking as a generative activity. *Journal of Educational Psychology, 70,* 514-522.

Silberman, M. L. (1996). *Active learning: 101 strategies to teach any subject.* Boston: Allyn & Bacon.

Singelis, T. M. (Ed.) (1998). *Teaching about culture, ethnicity, and diversity.* Thousand Oaks, CA: Sage Publications.

Svinicki, M. D. (1991). Practical implications of cognitive theories. *New Directions for Teaching and Learning, 45,* 27-37.

Weiland, A. & Kingsbury, S. J. (1979). Immediate and delayed recall of lecture material as a function of note taking. *Journal of Educational Research, 72,* 228-230.

Chapter 10

Affirmation Book Project: Impacting Diversity, Literacy, and Collaboration

Melinda K. Swafford
Rebekah A. Thomas
Sue Bailey

PURPOSE, OBJECTIVES, AND RATIONALE

Purpose

The purpose of the Affirmation Book Project was to:

- Create a climate within the family and consumer sciences (FACS) classroom that fostered an understanding of the international families within the community.
- Emphasize the concept of cultural sensitivity and respect for diversity while fostering collaboration among students, community partners, and families.
- Develop an educational tool that would benefit children enrolled in Head Start and their families with the essential task of parent/child reading.

Objectives

Upon completion of this teaching strategy, learners will be able to:

- Recognize the diversity of families within the community.
- Identify factors that place children at risk.

© 2006 by The Haworth Press, Inc. All rights reserved.
doi:10.1300/5609_10

- Understand the impact of parental involvement, specifically international families, upon emergent literacy and education.
- Identify how affirmation affects child development and family dynamics.
- Identify the importance of respectful collaboration among families, students, teachers, and community partners.

Rationale

Within the past two decades there has been a dramatic increase in the number of Hispanic families living in the United States (Bailey, Skinner, Rodriguez, Gut, & Correa, 1999). Many Hispanic families have moved into areas that have been predominantly Caucasian for generations. Usually, the members of Hispanic families do not understand English, making adjustment into the community, especially the educational system, difficult. Likewise, professionals, including educators within the community, are faced with the assimilation of an ever-increasing number of families who may hold cultural values, beliefs, preferences, and languages different from their own (Sexton, Lobman, Constans, Snyder, & Ernest, 1997).

Through education, individuals are exposed to a deeper understanding of the way people live (Baker, 1994). The education process begins by defining diversity and describing how it is integrated into our lives. Baker (1994) revealed that individuals who have been taught to appreciate diversity are more self-confident, have increased abilities, and move beyond judging individuals by superficial attributes such as skin color or speech patterns.

Reading skills provide the foundation for the academic success of children. Emergent literacy consists of the skills, knowledge, and attitudes that are developmental to conventional forms of reading and writing (Lonigan, et al., 1999). The goal of emergent literacy is to build an environment that is rich in print enabling young children to acquire basic literacy concepts and skills (Schuman & Reilhan, 1990). Research by Anderson (2000) revealed that parents, not the schools, lay the foundation for a child learning to read.

Parental involvement in learning and educational resources, such as literature in the home, appears to influence the academic success and the cognitive growth of the child. Factors that inhibit parental involvement include: race, poverty, mistrust, and language. Lack of exposure to literature activities is strongly associated with deficits in emergent literacy skills in children from low-income backgrounds (Lonigan et al., 1999). In addition, children with language and reading disabilities are at high risk for the development of social, behavioral, and emotional disabilities. These social and behavioral difficulties further impede academic success and make special education services more likely (Lonigan et al., 1999). Furthermore, children who speak English as a second language are at risk for delayed acquisition in reading skills (Golova, Alario, Vivier, Rodriguez, & High, 1999).

Parent-child reading activities represent a rich source of verbal interaction. In fact, when activities that provide language interaction such as playtime, mealtime, dressing, and reading have been compared, the greatest quantity and quality of parent-child interaction have been found during parent-child reading activities (Mendelsohn et al., 2001). Research reveals that parent-child reading activities increase success in oral language development, reading ability, and school performance for the child (Mendelsohn et al., 2001). Book sharing is one of the most emphasized activities in programs designed to maximize literacy development (Schuman & Reilhan, 1990). Book sharing is defined as an adult reading to the child in a warm, nurturing manner. The adult involves the child with the story and increases comprehension by asking questions. This concept can be difficult, if not impossible, for families that do not have books written in their native language.

Professionals, including educators, should plan ways to facilitate parent-child reading activities which promote and respect that parents are the first and foremost teachers of the child. A study conducted by Anderson (2000) on parental involvement of families from lower socioeconomic levels revealed that the majority of families felt reading was important, and over half of the families in the survey were good role models, i.e., reading in front of their children. When the school supplied reading materials, 100 percent of the students read with their parents. However, when the reading materials were not provided by the schools, the percentage of the students participating in reading activities were not as prevailing. This study highlighted the importance of developing strategies and projects to help families with the essential task of parent-child reading.

Blasi (2002) described a study that prepared individuals for teaching in a diverse and complicated society. A major goal of the study was for students to look at children and families and recognize strengths and potential instead of deficiencies. The study used the term "of promise" to define: children living in poverty, and children belonging to a cultural/ethnic minority, whose first language was one other than English, and whose family organizations may be nontraditional. The content of the study included involvement in literature study groups, which focused on family strengths and family use of literacy. The results indicated that students who participated in the study believe that developing a relationship of trust and understanding with families was the most important factor in family collaboration. Students need opportunities to participate in projects that allow for multiple interactions with children and families in order to build on home, school, and community experiences.

An article by Barillas (2000) indicated that teachers, child care providers, and professionals should make an effort to include parents in the classroom activities, regardless if the parent can speak English or not. Honoring parent voices creates an environment of collaboration between the family and the professional. When professionals and families speak different languages the task may be more complex. However, respectful collaboration between families and professionals can bridge language barriers.

PROCEDURE

The Affirmation Book Project was initiated in a family and consumer sciences—family dynamics/child development course. The class of eighteen high school students was inclusive and diverse. The diversity included academic ability, gender, and nationality. The majority of students had little or no experience with young children and several of the students commented that they had never heard of the term "affirmation" before the class began the project. The school is located in a predominately Caucasian Appalachian community in Tennessee with a population of 2,800. Approximately 560 people (20 percent) in the town are Hispanic, most of who have moved into the area within the past five years. The rural community is of low socioeconomic status.

The young children involved in the Affirmation Book Project attended the local Head Start program. Most were of low socioeconomic status and several had diagnosed disabilities. The majority of the preschool children who had a diagnosed disability had deficits in the area of speech and language. One-third of the young children were Hispanic. Many parents of the young Hispanic children could not speak English.

The Head Start Program, established in 1965, was the first federal program committed to the well-being of at-risk children, ages three to five, who meet federal poverty guidelines (Bailey, 2000). Head Start programs provide concrete learning experiences in all the developmental domains with emphasis on emergent literacy and concrete experiences. In 1972, federal law mandated that 10 percent of the children served by Head Start Programs have a diagnosed disability (Bailey, 2000).

The term "affirmation" was defined and the importance of affirmation in the life of a child was discussed. The high school students researched the critical role affirmation plays in the development of a child. The students found that affirmation is a term most often used in denoting positive verbal proclamation of the worth and value of an individual. Specifically, *Webster's II New College Dictionary* (Berube, 2001, p. 19) defines affirm as, "to strengthen, declare, or maintain, to be true—to ratify." The students then discussed the relationship between affirmation and high self-esteem, self-worth, and self-acceptance. The need for parental involvement in the life of the child was discussed, and the high school students became aware of the positive impact that results from parents reading to their child.

The high school students researched factors that place children at risk. They discovered that the impact of poverty on children is likely to include lack of school readiness skills, delayed growth and development, and increased grade retention or failure to complete high school. The students compared their findings concerning at-risk factors to the characteristics of the children at the Head Start Center. The students noted the challenges the children faced in comparison with other children their ages. It was determined that the children at the Head Start Center faced a more challenging future and were considered part of the at-risk population. In particular, the Hispanic children faced additional challenges since English was not the dominant language spoken in the home. The FACS students decided that affirmation should be a significant factor in each child's life.

Students became aware of research related to the significance of reading in the life of a child. Research conducted by Golova et al.

(1999) noted that reading aloud is an important activity to prepare children to succeed in learning to read. Students learned that reading failure disproportionately affects children from socially and economically disadvantaged groups and contributes to the propagation of the cycle of poverty (Anastasiow, Levine-Hanes, & Hanes, 1982). Since the Head Start Center had several children whose primary language was Spanish, the FACS students decided that many Hispanic children were at risk for reading difficulties and school failure (Golova et al., 1999). In addition, research by Jimenez (2003) revealed that Hispanic students respond favorably to instruction that combines developmentally appropriate practices with innovative bilingual projects.

It was determined that the students would develop a teaching tool that would affirm the child, respect the diversity of the child and family, and promote parent-child reading. The FACS students began the Affirmation Book Project by volunteering two days per week at the Head Start Center and were assigned two to three children. Each student was required to spend one and a half hours with the children at each visit. The students kept journals, which included specific attributes, characteristics, interests, and abilities of each child. After approximately four weeks, the high school students created an affirmation book for each child.

Criteria were established for the Affirmation Book Project with student input. The criteria ensured that each child would receive a book of high quality and with educational value. The criteria included information regarding the book size, number of pages, type of cover, binding techniques, picture requirements, educational value requirement, and information concerning color and texture. Students were encouraged to be creative and to include the name of the child on each page.

The FACS students wrote and illustrated an affirmation book for each child. The content affirmed the many positive qualities and attributes of the child that the FACS student observed during the four weeks of interaction. To make the books bilingual, the students who were Hispanic, collaborated with students whose primary language was English. The students read the Affirmation Book to the children. The book was then given to the child to take home for the parent and child to read together.

ASSESSING EFFECTIVENESS

This innovative bilingual project addressed factors associated with lack of international parental involvement in literature activities, mainly language. The Affirmation Book Project combined many characteristics of current research when working with diverse and at-risk families in promoting emergent literacy. Translating the books into Spanish allowed the Hispanic families to participate in book sharing and develop warm, rich verbal interaction with their children. In addition, as part of the project, students were required to keep a journal on their thoughts and experiences of working with the children of the Head Start program. Responses from the high school students about the Affirmation Book Project were positive. Comments from students participating in the project follow.

Each page represented something special about each child. As the pages turned, their self-esteem grew. We strived to increase their confidence. Our goal was successfully met. We walked away feeling heroic because we made a difference in a child's life.

It was great having the book written in both [English and Spanish] languages. The parents could read this to their children at home. The parents also had the benefits of learning a new language and culture. I also learned a lot about the children and their culture. We are more alike than different.

It's different than you think. It's exciting. It brings our textbook to life. It's much more fun to learn about something in the class and then get to actually see it in real life. This project helped me connect class work to real life.

I really enjoyed every part of the [Affirmation Book] project. The best part was giving the children their own individual book. It touched me to see the smiles on each child's face. Each child wanted me to read his or her book over and over to them. Each time I read the book to the child, his or her smile became brighter and bigger. I believe each child enjoyed their own individual book as much as I enjoyed making it.

Responses were elicited from the staff and family members of the children involved in the project. Comments from the staff and family members were also positive:

It was a wonderful project. The students from the high school worked individually with the children and formed a relationship with the children. Books were made for each individual child, which depicted favorite toys, activities, and areas of strengths in the child. If the children were Hispanic, the books were written in both English and Spanish. Most importantly the children were able to take the books home to share with their family. This is a wonderful way to involve parents in their child's education.

What a great project! The high school students made a book for each child in the center. The day the high school students gave the books to the children was an exciting day. Each child was amazed that the book was all about them and only them. The children were able to take the books home and share with their parents. It was a great way to have parent involvement.

My younger sister is so proud of her book. She wants it read to her each day. It is pinned on the wall in our bedroom. My mother can read the book since it is written in Spanish. This book is helping my mother learn English.

CONCLUSION

The Affirmation Book Project was successful in creating a climate that fostered multicultural understanding. The books, a collaborative project between a high school family and consumer science class and the local Head Start program, were given to all families in order to increase involvement in the education of their child. This project provided a vehicle for all families, including international families, for quality parent-child reading, thus enhancing the emergent literacy skills of the children. In addition, the esteem of the child was enhanced through the sharing of the Affirmation Book each time it was read. By devoting a book to each child, the project affirmed the experience, culture, and language of the children and their specific families. Most important, the Affirmation Book Project instilled in the high school student awareness and respect for diversity.

REFERENCES

Anastasiow, N.J., Levine-Hanes, M., & Hanes, M.L. (1982). *Language and reading strategies for poverty children*. Baltimore, MD: University Park.

Anderson, S.A. (2000). How parental involvement makes a difference in reading achievement. *Reading Improvement, 37(2)*, 61-85.

Bailey, D.B., (2000). The federal role in early intervention: Prospect for the future. *Topics in Early Childhood Special Education, 20(2)*, 71-82.

Bailey, D.B., Skinner, D., Rodriguez, P., Gut, D., & Correa, V. (1999). Awareness, use, and satisfaction with services for Latino parents of young children with disabilities. *Exceptional Children, 65(3)*, 367-389.

Baker, G.C. (1994). Teaching children to respect diversity. *Childhood Education, 71(1)*, 33-36.

Barillas, M.R. (2000). Literacy at home: Honoring parent voices through writing. *The Reading Teacher, 54(3)*, 302-309.

Berube, M.S. (Ed.). (2001). *Webster's II new college dictionary.* New York, NY: Houghton Mifflin Co.

Blasi, M.W. (2002). An asset model: Preparing pre-service teacher to work with children and families "of promise." *Journal of Research in Childhood Education, 17(1)*, 106-122.

Golova, N., Alario, A.J., Vivier, P.M., Rodriguez, M., & High, P.C. (1999). Literacy promotion for Hispanic families in a primary care setting: A randomized controlled trial. *Pediatrics, 103(5)*, 993-994.

Jimenez, R.T. (2003). Literacy and Latino students in the United States: Some considerations, questions, and new directions. *Reading Research Quarterly, 38(1)*, 122-130.

Lonigan, C.J., Bloomfield, B.G., Anthony, J.L., Bacon, K.D., Phillips, B.M., & Samwel, C.S. (1999). Relations among emergent literacy skills, behavior problems, and social competence in preschool children from low and middle income backgrounds. *Topics in Early Childhood Special Education, 19(1)*, 40-49.

Mendelsohn, A.L., Mogilner, L.N., Dreyer, B.P., Forman, J.A., Weinstein, S.C., Broderick, M., Cheng, K.J., Magloire, T., & Napier, C. (2001). The impact of clinic-based literacy intervention on language development in inner city preschool children, *Pediatrics, 107(1)*, 130-141.

Schuman, D.R. & Reilhan, J. (1990). The caregiver's role in emergent literacy. *Children Today, 19(20)*, 20-26.

Sexton, D., Lobman, M., Constans, T., Snyder, P., & Ernest, J. (1997). Early interventionists' perspective of multicultural practices with African American families. *Exceptional Children, 63(3)*, 313-329.

Chapter 11

Creating an Electronic Portfolio to Integrate Multiculturism in Teaching Family Economics

Anita M. Subramaniam

PURPOSE, OBJECTIVES, AND RATIONALE

Purpose

The purpose of creating an electronic portfolio to integrate multi-culturism in teaching family economics includes:

- Introducing and developing technological skills in teaching and learning
- Creating a product that can be stored, modified, and reused for future educational purposes
- Creating an exercise that involves teamwork
- Facilitating learning through utilization of interactive media and sharing of knowledge between team members, classmates, and to a larger audience via the Internet

Objectives

Upon completion of this learning activity, students will be able to:

- Create electronic portfolios
- Learn and utilize technological skills that will be useful to them in various ways
- Learn to work in a team

doi:10.1300/5609_11

- Build relationships, appreciate, and take advantage of one another's assets to produce best results
- Effectively utilize the Internet to search and access information on economic aspects of families in other countries
- Distinguish what is authentic and reliable information on the Internet
- Select, organize, and present information to learn and inform others in class about families in countries that they have chosen to study
- Share electronic documents with other students via e-mail or by publishing them on the Web or via Blackboard.

Rationale

The rationale of using electronic media to teach multiculturalism is fivefold. First, creating an opportunity to use technology makes students more marketable. Technological skills have become a necessity in the workplace and therefore students with these skills are at a competitive advantage in the labor marketplace.

Second, in today's modern age, most information is available online. Most students are adept in using the Internet and find useful information easily. Those students who are not adept in using the Internet, will learn to use it for finding information. The exercise also creates an opportunity to teach students to distinguish what is reliable and authentic information versus that which is not.

Third, creating a portfolio enables students to brainstorm, utilizing their creative skills. Students enjoy the hands-on experience of using their artistic and creative ideas in creating a document.

Fourth, students are able to download and add colorful images and links from Web sites to their documents. Students often do a good job of creating an electronic portfolio, as this is a skill that many students either already possess or are interested in learning. Most students use the Internet for many educational and leisure purposes.

Last, but not of any less importance, is creating a project that involves teamwork. There are several benefits of teamwork. Most important, it enables students to learn from one another, share skills and knowledge that enrich the end product, and develop interrelationship skills.

PROCEDURE

Students form groups of three or four and select a country about which they would like to learn. Once the selection is made, students collect as much information as is available. Following is an example of an outline that can be used to organize information.

1. Introduction
   Location of the country
   World map
   Country map
   Flag, national anthem, emblems, brief history
   Land area
2. People
   Lifestyle
   Religions
   Clothing
   Customs and traditions
   Food
3. Political and economic systems
   Type of political system (capitalism, communism, monarchy, military rule, etc. along with present political leaders' names)
   Type of economic system, currency, gross national product, major industries, items of export and import, and similar facts
   Special facts about the country with relation to the world such as the third-most populous country in the world, first country to introduce democracy, etc.
4. Culture of families
   Living arrangement of families (e.g., nuclear, extended, three generation, etc.)
   Role distribution within family
   Social norms and customs with regard to events such as marriages, childbirth, death, divorce, and other facts considered important in that country
5. Economic data
   Total population, population density
   Gender and age distribution of the population

Life expectancy, birth rates, death rates, and infant mortality rates
Educational attainment and literacy rates of the population
Labor force participation rates by gender
Per-capita income
Income differentials
6. Present information on any one of the following
Housing
Health
Consumption patterns
Financial management

Students create an electronic portfolio using Microsoft Power-Point presentation and FrontPage, FrontPage is Microsoft's Web page editor. Technology specialists in the college or the university may be invited to teach skills related to creating an electronic portfolio. The technology specialist may cover the following topics:

1. Creating a PowerPoint presentation
Opening a new document, keying information, using different slide layouts
Creating charts and tables
Inserting images from clip art
Using Clip art and downloading Clip art from "free" sources
Using themes and backgrounds
Using different transitions and sound
Organizing slides through sorting, viewing, saving, printing, making changes
Downloading video and audio clips from the Internet and using in PowerPoint presentation
2. Using digital video cameras
Basic operation and functions of a video camera
Recording a video clip
Editing and transferring the video clip to a computer
Creating digital video clips and inserting in PowerPoint presentation
3. Using FrontPage
Opening a new Web document using FrontPage

Creating a Web document that has tables, titles, an introduction, link to the main course page, and the PowerPoint Presentation along with other digital images
Saving, editing, and formatting Web documents
4. Publishing the electronic portfolio on Blackboard and the Web.

A librarian may be invited to inform students of the library's resources and ways to use its online search engines to gather information. Specifically, the librarian may share information on:

1. The different library resources available through the multimedia center, reference desk, circulation desk, government document section, computer center, and others of relevance.
2. Using the library's computers and offline computers to search and retrieve information on families in other countries; using the Internet to search for information; the different search engines and search terms that can be used to retrieve information; navigating through web pages; identifying authentic sources of information; copyright regulations and concerns in using online materials.
3. Resources to use for learning about American Psychological Association (APA) format for online and offline materials.

Some of the basic economic concepts and principles that the students will encounter while performing this project have to be covered in the class prior to commencement of the project. These may include concepts such as: household as a consuming unit; demand and supply; types of goods; types of markets; types of economic systems; pricing in competitive markets; income of families in the United States and factors that affect economic status etc; American families and home ownership; comparison of economic status of single parents and married couples/families; economic status of single custodial parents; poverty in American families; and American consumption patterns.

Students may be given class time to discuss the distribution of group members' efforts and plan their work. Students may also be allowed to spend at least two class sessions in the library to perform group work together. The instructor's periodic interaction with each group to ensure students are working well together, that they are not faced with any challenges, and that they are progressing in their work according to time schedule may be important.

Examples

In the past students have studied the lifestyle and economic data of families of the following countries: Canada, China, Denmark, Egypt, England, France, Germany, India, Italy, Japan, Mexico, Portugal, Senegal, South Korea, and Spain.

The United States Census Bureau's Web site (www.census.gov) is used extensively in the course. The American FactFinder (http://factfinder.census.gov) and Census publications are used to learn about the United States. The Census Bureau International Data base is used to retrieve basic data such as population, population density, growth rate, death rate, infant mortality rate, migration rate. Other Internet sources such as the following are listed on Blackboard for students to visit and obtain information on the country that they are studying. Students are also required to search other sources for information.

Internet Sources for Students

Educational Institutions

A National Survey of Families and Households. The Center of Demography and Ecology at the University of Wisconsin collects data on families and households including the respondent's family living arrangements in childhood, departures and returns to the parental home, and histories of marriage, cohabitation, education, fertility, and employment. Further information is available at http://www.ssc.wisc .edu/cde/library/cderr/subscribe.htm and http://www.ssc.wisc.edu/cde/nsfhwp/home.htm.

Population and Development Program. This is at the Department of Development Sociology at the Cornell University. The Web site provides links to various Population Resources. Further information is available at http:www.einaudi.cornell.edu/pdp/resources/index .asp and http:www.einaudi.cornell.edu/pdp/.

Penn State Social Science Research Institute. This provides a list of links to various government, educational, and nongovernmental agencies that publish information on families. Also provides a list of universities that have a center on demographic studies. Links provided to: Princeton University Office of Population Research; RAND Population Research Center; SUNY Albany Center for Social and Demographic Analysis; UCLA California Center for Population Research; University of Chicago Population Research Center; University of Maryland Population Research Center; University of Michigan Population Studies Center; University of Minnesota Population Center; University of North Carolina Population Center; University of Pennsylvania Population Studies Center; University of Texas at Austin Population Research Center; University of Washington Center for Studies in Demography and Ecology; University of Wisconsin-Madison Center for Demography and Ecology. Further information is available at http://athens.pop.psu.edu/allen/LinksByCat .cfm?SubjectID=6.

International Nonprofit Organizations

United Nations Population Information Network (POPIN). This provides a guide to population information on U.N. system Web sites.

United Nations Population Division - Department of Economic and Social Affairs. The Statistics Division of the U.N. Population Information Network provides information on demography and social statistics on families and households, health, housing, education, social welfare, income and consumption, and basic population parameters such as population, birth rate, death rate, life expectancy, etc. Further information is available at http://unstats.un.org/unsd/demographic/ sconcerns/fam/default.htm and http://www.un.org/popin/.

UNFPA. The United Nations Population Fund (UNFPA), is an international development agency that promotes the right of every woman, man, and child to enjoy a life of health and equal opportunity. UNFPA supports countries in using population data for policies and programs to reduce poverty and to ensure that every pregnancy is wanted, every birth is safe, every young person is free of HIV/AIDS, and every girl and woman is treated with dignity and respect. Further information is available at http://www.unfpa.org/.

UNICEF. Provides information on children. Information is categorized by countries and regions. Further information is available at http://www.unicef.org/infobycountry/index.html and http://www .unicef.org/.

The World Bank. The World Bank's annual World Development Report (WDR) is an invaluable guide to the economic, social, and environmental state of the world today. Each year the WDR provides in-depth analysis of a specific aspect of development. Past reports have considered such topics as the role of the state, transition economies, labor, infrastructure, health, the environment, and poverty.

World Development Indicators (WDI) is the World Bank's premier annual compilation of data about development. Further information is available at http://www.worldbank.org/.

World Health Organization (WHO). The Web site provides health indicators by country. Further information is available at http://www.who.int/countries/en/ and http://www.who.int/en/.

United States Government Agencies

U.S. Bureau of the Census. The U.S. Bureau of the Census, part of the Department of Commerce, collects and publishes data on the United States and other countries of the world. Economic indicators, population parameters, and wide range of data are provided. Further information is available at www.census.gov.

Data Online for Population, Health and Nutrition. The Data Online for Population, Health and Nutrition (DOLPHN) is an online statistical data resource of selected demographic and health indicators gathered from various sources for several countries of the world. It is driven by USAID (United States Agency for International Development). Further information is available at http://www.phnip.com/dolphn/.

Social Statistics Briefing Room. The White House provides current social statistics with key demographic indicators such as current population of the United States and the world; household income; poverty; household wealth; earnings and field of degree; health indicators such as life expectancy; health care coverage; health behaviors (alcohol use, smoking, etc); and education indicators such as international comparison in sience and math, reading achievement, math achievement, trends in women's education, etc. Further information is available at http://www.whitehouse.gov/fsbr/ssbr.html.

National Center for Education Statistics (NCES). Part of the U.S. Department of Education. Further information is available at http://www.nces.ed.gov.

United States Agency for International Development (USAID). USAID provides information predominantly on challenges faced by each country and the role of the United States in overcoming these challenges. Further information is available at http://www/usaid.gov.

Centers for Disease Control and Prevention (CDC). The Centers for Disease Control and Prevention provides data through its Data and Statistics center on various health issues facing Americans. Further information is available at http://www.cdc.gov/.

National Center for Health Statistics (NCHS). NCHS, which is a part of the CDC, provides data and statistics on health parameters of Americans. Further information is available at http://www.dcd.gov/ nchs/hus.htm.

National Institutes of Health (NIH). The U.S. Department of Health and Human Services provides information on health issues. Further information is available at http://www.nih.gov.

National Center on Minority Health and Health Disparities (NCMHD). Further information is available at http://www.ncmhd. nih.gov.

National Institute of Child Health and Human Development (NICHD). Further information is available at http://www.nichd.nih. gov.

National Institute of Child Health & Human Development (NICHD). Demographic and Behavioral Sciences Branch (DBS) information available at http://www.nichd.nih.gov/about/cpr/dbs/dbs. htm.

National Institute on Aging (NIA). Further information is available at http://www.nia.nih.gov.

Bureau of Labor Statistics. The Bureau of Labor Statistics of the U.S. Department of Labor provides information on employment and unemployment rates in the United States; inflation and consumer spending; wages, earning, and benefits; occupation-related data; international economic data; demographic data of the labor force; and consumption data in the United States. Further information is available at www.bls.gov.

International

Vienna Institute of Demography. Provides demography of Austria, comparative demography of European nations, population forecast and others. Further information available at http://www.oeaw.ac.at/vid.

Australian National University. Demography and Population Studies Provides links to a variety of population information. Further information is available at http://dempgraphy.anu.edu.au/VirtualLibrary/.

The CIA World Fact Book. The Central Intelligence Agency publishes a fact book every year on information on essential facts about different countries. Flags, culture, history, people, etc., are available online at http://www.odci.gov/cia/publications/factbook/index.html.

The World Fact Book. Provides demographic information by country and the latest news about people. Further information is available at http://factbook.wn.com/.

The WashingtonPost.com. Provides world news and search engine to obtain information on different countries. Further information is available at http://www.washingtonpost.com/wp-dyn/world/search/.

World Facts US. Provides information on different countries. Further information is available at http://worldfacts.us/.

ASSESSMENT AND EVALUATION

In the past I have received feedback from students and peers on using technology to promote learning. Students may be asked to evaluate the tool with respect to learning new technology, learning about global families, and in working as a team. Specifically, students may be asked to answer the following questions anonymously:

1. What are some perceivable benefits of learning to create an electronic portfolio?
2. What are some skills you did not know and which you learned through this class?
   Creating PowerPoint Presentation
   Creating a Web document using FrontPage
   Publishing Web documents
   Using a digital camera
   Creating a digital video clip
   Searching the Internet for information
   Downloading clip art and video/audio clips and attaching to a document
   Sharing the document with other students via electronic media
   Learning about library resources

Using library resources
Searching information on the Internet
Using search engines, and using search terms
Identifying authentic and reliable sources of online information
Using APA format
Copyright regulations and plagiarism
3. Did you find the demonstrations by the technology specialist and the librarian useful in fulfilling the requirements of this exercise? If no, state how this can be improved.
4. Did you benefit from using technology to learn about families in other nations? If yes, how did you benefit? If no, why not?
5. Did you find using the Internet an easy way to gather information on families in the country you chose to study? If yes, please specify the Internet sites you visited and the country you studied. If no, state other resources you used to gather information along with the country you studied.
6. Did you enjoy teamwork? What are some skills you developed or new knowledge you gained by working as a team? What were the challenges?
7. Do you have any comments or suggestions to improve this project?

The Internet is a very useful tool in acquiring information on global families and economic data. Students are very creative in organizing and using different clipart and images in making presentations colorful and interesting. Most students came to the class without knowing how to create a PowerPoint Presentation. Although not all students mastered the technology, they all learned the basic concepts.

ASSESSING STUDENT PERFORMANCE

In assessing student performance, students are evaluated on their participation and involvement in teamwork, regularity in attendance of group meetings, skillfulness in use of technology, and presentation skills. Team members are asked for their feedback on group work. Confidentiality in information they provide is maintained. Skillfulness in using technology and presentation of the information are assessed as a group. Exhibit 11.1 shows the form used for assessment.

EXHIBIT 11.1 Course Assessment Table

	Presentation skill: Clarity, speed, time	Graphics and Pictures, Font (visual appeal)	Depth (information)	Organization of information	Citations of external sources
Introduction: Location of the country World map Country map Flag, national anthem, emblems, brief history					
People: the religions, clothing, customs and traditions, food					
Political and economic systems: type of political system and economic system, currency, gross national product, major industries, items of export and import, and similar facts					
Culture of families: living arrangement of families (e.g., nuclear, extended, three generation, etc.), role distribution within family, social norms and customs with regard to events such as marriages, childbirth, death, divorce, and others considered important in that country					
Economic data: Total population, population density Gender and age distribution of the population					
Life expectancy, birth rates, death rates, and infant mortality rates					
Educational attainment and literacy rates of the population					
Labor force participation rates by gender					

Per-capita income, income differentials					
Present information on any one of the following: Housing Health Consumption patterns Financial management					
Reference list (APA format)					

E = Excellent, G = Good, F = Fair, S = Satisfactory, P = Poor

Contextual learning about families in different countries is important. People live differently in different parts of the world. Examining families in other parts of the world not only helps us gain an appreciation of diversity, but also enables us to understand and appreciate lifestyle variances, causes for those differences, and economic factors that give rise to those causes. This course enhances cultural understanding, as well as lays a foundation for students to be able to work with people from and in different countries.

Chapter 12

Communicating Across Preferences: A Comparative Family Systems Example

Ann Creighton-Zollar

PURPOSE, OBJECTIVES, AND RATIONALE

Purpose

The major purposes of the project are:

- Teach students how to use an important electronic resource for the comparative study of family systems.
- Increase the ability of students to function effectively in small collaborative work groups by enhancing their ability to communicate across learning preferences.
- Provide students with the opportunity to prepare, present, and participate in a multisensory kinetic learning experience.

Objectives

Upon completion of the class projects students should:

- Know what data from the Human Relations Area File (HRAF) are available in the library on microfiche and what HRAF data are available in electronic formats.
- Be able to use a personal computer to access a subset of HRAF data that are available electronically and called eHRAF.

doi:10.1300/5609_12

189

- Demonstrate the ability to use eHRAF resources to compare and contrast two family systems along the dimensions presented in the outline that follows and write a traditional "term paper" based on that outline.
- Understand their own preferences for sending and receiving information and how their ability to communicate effectively is enhanced when they attend to the preferences of others.
- Be able to use graphical organizer software to prepare electronic reports that suit diverse preferences.
- Be able to prepare and deliver a live, multisensory, kinesthetic presentation.

Rationale

The activities described in this chapter are used in an upper division, undergraduate course on comparative family systems for students who are seeking to earn degrees in sociology and anthropology. Over the past fifty years it has become a standard practice to ask students in this type of course to learn about and use the HRAF (Ember & Ember, 1997). In this course, emphasis is placed on using the subset of the HRAF data available in electronic format, which is called eHRAF (Ember & Cunnar, 2003). Many of the students who take this course plan to become teachers. The emphasis on eHRAF is consistent with the national goals of helping these future teachers to be ready to effectively use computers in their classrooms. Although graphical organizers are more heavily used in K-12 education than in higher education, they have the potential to enhance learning at all levels.

Teachers have assumed that students learn best when they are actively involved in their own learning. The visual, aural, read/write and kinesthetic (VARK) learning preference Web site (www.vark-learn.com) provides all students, regardless of their career objectives, with a way to reflect upon their own learning and offers a list of specific activities through which they can maximize their own learning (Fleming, 2001). An important corollary to the active learning approach is that, where possible, it should involve small collaborative work groups. Unfortunately, many students do not know how to collaborate effectively and many professors do not know how to teach collaborative skills. The use of VARK learning preferences can help to mitigate these problems because it also allows students to reflect upon the diverse ways in which their classmates prefer to send and receive information and to see how that diversity can strengthen group performance. The VARK learning preferences help students to understand the benefits of attending to the learning preferences of others and thereby provide an opportunity for them to increase their ability to work collaboratively (Fleming, 1995).

The VARK learning preferences have implications that go well beyond the classroom. VARK provides people with insight into how they prefer to send information and how they prefer to receive information. These preferences for sending and receiving information are just as important in one's professional and personal lives as they are in the classroom. People who have the capacity to attend to how others prefer to receive information and the ability to adjust their messages accordingly will be more effective communicators in many types of professional and personal situations.

VARK identifies four preferences: visual images, aural, reading/ writing, and kinesthetic. The visual preference (V) includes the diagrammatic material that is often used by teachers to symbolize information (e.g., graphs, charts, flow charts, models, and all the symbolic arrows, circles, hierarchies, and other devices used to represent information). The second perceptual mode, aural (A), describes a preference for "heard" information. Students with an aural preference report that they learn best from lectures, tutorials, and discussions. Third, some students prefer to learn from information that is composed primarily of printed words (R). For the purposes of the questionnaire, the fourth perceptual mode, kinesthetic (K), is defined as the perceptual preference related to the use of experience and practice (simulated or real). Experience and practice may involve using sight, touch, taste, smell, and hearing. A kinesthetic teaching experience uses one or more of these perceptual modes to connect the student to reality. The teacher may be presenting information visually (V), aurally (A), or in a read/write fashion (R), but the experience is kinesthetic because of the integrative and real nature of the information.

Once students understand the learning preferences identified through VARK, they easily see how graphical organizer software facilities communication across visual, auditory, and read-write preferences. Graphical organizer software provides a means through which information entered through the graphic interface can be read in outline or text format. It also allows you to use the graphic interface to view information entered as text. The sound utilities in the software allow the user to hear the machine read all of the information in the file aloud. Many students are not sure that they understand the kinesthetic learning preference until they complete their in-class presentations.

My initial rationale for asking students to make their in-class presentations multisensory and kinesthetic was the desire to beat the "end-of-the-semester doldrums." I teach this course each spring semester. Over the years, I had come to recognize that the standard approaches to the end-of-the-semester presentations were excruciatingly boring. Student attendance always went down during presentation weeks. Dull, repetitive presentations in the classroom were competing with the most beautiful days of spring outside. Unless I drastically increased the contribution that attendance made to their grades, students would not show up to listen to the presentations of others. The only ones who came were those that were feeling stress and anxiety about their final grades. The idea for the multisensory presentations began when I started each class presentation day with deep-breathing exercises and provided the students cold drinks, healthy snacks, and hand fans. The students responded by bringing things to their presentations that they wanted their classmates to experience.

PROCEDURES

A. Have students complete the online VARK questionnaire to determine their own learning preference profile and report their scores to the instructor.
   1. Discuss the diverse learning preference profiles of the class members.
   2. Ask students to reflect upon how differences in learning preferences affect interactions at home, in school, and in the workplace.
B. Assign students to work groups comprised of members with diverse learning preferences and ask them to collaborate on the class project.
C. The class project
   1. Each group must select two family systems for a comparative analysis. Students are encouraged to select cultures for which data are available through eHRAF.

2. The students must compare and contrast the family systems and the cultural groups to which they belong along the following dimensions, the first nine of which are available in the eHRAF cultural summaries.

D. Dimensions of Family Systems
   1. Ethnonyms
   2. Orientation
      a. Identification and location
      b. Demography
      c. Linguistic affiliation
   3. History and cultural affiliations
   4. Settlement
   5. Economy
      a. Subsistence
      b. Industrial arts
      c. Trade
      d. Division of labor
      e. Land tenure
   6. Sociopolitical organization
      a. Social organization
      b. Political organization
      c. Social control
      d. Conflict
   7. Religion and expressive culture
      a. Religious beliefs
      b. Religious practitioners
      c. Ceremonies
      d. Medicine
      e. Death and afterlife
   8. Kinship
      a. Kin groups and descent
      b. Kinship terminology
   9. Marriage and family
      a. Marriage
      b. Domestic unit
      c. Inheritance
  10. The impact of social change
      a. The industrial revolution
      b. The digital revolution

      i. Information technology
     ii. Biogenetics
  E. Students prepare their complete analyses using graphical organizer software and post the electronic file to the course Blackboard for review by the entire class and for grading by the professor.
    1. The graphical organizer software allows the report to be seen as a diagram, read as text, and heard as a sound file.
    2. Some groups create Web sites and/or PowerPoint Presentations in addition to their graphical organizer files.
  F. The Kinesthetic "Multisensory" Presentation

During the last two weeks of the semester, the collaborative work groups present one of the family systems that they have studied. These presentations do not involve the group members standing in front of the class taking turns reading to us from PowerPoint slides. These presentations do not require the groups to recite every fact or statistic they have learned about the family system as rapidly as possible. The goals of these presentations are to teach us one or two things about the family system as vividly and deeply as possible and thereby encourage us to learn more. These presentations are kinesthetic, multisensory experiences involving sight, sound, touch, taste, and smell.

CLASS PROJECT EXAMPLE:
THE DOGON AND ASHANTI AFRICAN CULTURES

After logging on to eHRAF, the members of one collaborative work group decided that their class project would focus on two African cultures: the Dogon, who live largely in the country of Mali, and the Ashanti of Ghana. Because the written part of the assignment is structured to match the organization of the eHRAF cultural summaries, the initial comparative analysis simply required them to follow the outline (presented in the last section) in a very straightforward way. The students also found it easy to enter the information into the graphical organizer and to upload that file to the course Blackboard so that every student in the class had access to their report.

The collaborative work group then had to decide whether their class presentation would focus on the Dogon or the Ashanti and what lesson they would teach the class. After a series of discussions the group decided that they would present the Ashanti. They elected to present the Ashanti for two reasons. First of all, they wanted to teach a lesson about the types of conflict that can arise when matrilineal descent is coupled with patrilocal residence. The Ashanti trace descent through the mother's line. At certain points in the life cycle, Ashanti residential units can contain a woman, her children, and her husband and be located in proximity to the matrilineage to which the husband belongs. A matrilineage is a multigenerational group of relatives related by matrileneal descent.

The group also selected the Ashanti because they realized that they had easy access to artifacts reflective of Ashanti culture. One member of the group was surprised to discover that an old family recipe for "chicken with peanuts," which she had always thought of as southern, was identical to a Ghanaian recipe for groundnut stew. Another realized that in their travels his parents had acquired a collection that included Ashanti fertility dolls, hand-carved stools, beads, and drums. The entire group was intrigued by Ashanti proverbs and *adinkra* symbols. They thought that everyone in the class would recognize *kente* cloth because of the extent to which it has been adopted as a cultural symbol by African Americans.

On the day of their presentation, this group entered the room accompanied by the sound of an Ashanti "talking drum" and wearing clothes based on traditional Ashanti designs. Around the room they displayed Ashanti pottery, beadwork, stools, and other useful items carved from wood. They served their classmates small bowls of groundnut stew. They gave their classmates three types of cloth to examine. First, they gave them a tablecloth available from almost any department store with a *kente* design printed or stamped on one side. Then, they passed out examples of the exquisite *kente* traditionally woven by Ashanti men.

As their classmates were eating (smelling and tasting) the groundnut stew and looking at and touching the cloth, the members of the group started to perform a skit. In this skit they illustrated how patrilocal residence and matrilineal descent can create conflict. In the skit, a man who is husband to one woman and brother to another is being prepared for burial while his wife and his sister argue over his possessions. Portions of the argument were conducted by speaking in proverbs. A member of the group displayed the *adinkra* symbol for each proverb as it was spoken. In the skit, the women argue about who owns the house and the land. They are arguing about who owns the peanuts and the chickens, the cloth, and the drums. The members of the presenting group ask their classmates to adjudicate the disputes over some specific items. In order to do this, the members of the class must recognize the basic principle: property the man inherited from his matrilineage should go to his sisters' children but that the wife and her children have the right to those possessions that they helped him to acquire. In closing, this group invites the class to join them for further discussion on the course Blackboard where a heated debate has been taking place about the relative merits of the various ways in which human beings trace descent. The group's presentation definitely added more fuel to the debate.

ASSESSMENT RESULTS

The summer of 2007 will provide me with my first opportunity to examine the extent to which the use of the graphical organizer enhances learning. However, I do have some feedback on the effectiveness of several components of this class project. For example, the syllabus includes a statement that says this course provides reasonable accommodations to students if they provide a formal letter from the office that provides services to students with disabilities. Every semester several students without a formal diagnosis will tell me, "I think that I am dyslexic." These students usually say that they are unable to afford the testing. I point them toward affordable testing and the VARK assignment. After they have completed this class, many of these students come back to me with changed minds. These students see the issue facing them as one of learning preferences rather than learning disabilities. They express appreciation that someone has taken the time to help them understand their preferences and provide some concrete actions that they can take to improve their approach to studying. Other students offer positive comments about attending to the preferences of their spouses, their children, the children they teach, their co-workers, and their employers.

The multisensory final presentations have definitely cut down on the end-of-the-spring-semester doldrums. Attendance during the presentations has soared without the need for more stringent monitoring. Students come because they have discovered that their classmates are creative and talented and can contribute to their education in ways that are interesting and entertaining. They come because they discover that their classmates either come from or have visited interesting places and have interesting things for them to see, touch, and taste. They come because they do not want to miss the experience. The end-of-semester stress level has been greatly reduced. On the last day of the presentations, I must actually remind students that there is still a final exam to take and that they need to study each group's entire report. The overall final grades for the class have improved as well.

REFERENCES

Ember, C.R. & Cunnar, C. (2003). *Introduction to teaching eHRAF*. Retrieved October 14, 2003, from HRAF at Yale University Web site http://www.yale.edu/hraf/teaching.htm.

Ember, C.R. & Ember, M. (1997). *User's guide: HRAF collection of ethnography: A basic guide to cross-cultural research*. [Electronic Version]. Retrieved October 14, 2003, from HRAF at Yale University Web site http://www.yale.edu/hraf/publications.htm.

Fleming, N.D. (1995). I'm different; not dumb: Modes of presentation (VARK) in the tertiary classroom. In A. Zelmer (Ed.), *Research and development in higher education,* Proceedings of the 1995 Annual Conference of the Higher Education and Research Development Society of Australia (HERDSA), HERDSA, Vol. 18, (pp. 308-313). Retrieved October 14, 2003, from http://www.vark-learn.com/ documents/different_not_dumb.pdf.

Fleming, N. (2001). *VARK: A guide to learning styles.* Retrieved October 14, 2003, from http://www.vark-learn.com/english/index.asp.

Chapter 13

Using Cross-Cultural Travel Courses to Teach About International Families

Raeann R. Hamon
Cherie K. Fernsler

PURPOSE, OBJECTIVES, AND RATIONALE

Purpose

- To prepare future family professionals to work with culturally diverse populations and to increase their global perspective and awareness
- To incorporate experiential opportunities designed to help students understand and develop an appreciation for families and cultures different than their own
- To learn about the various facets of families in the host culture, including family cohesion, composition, roles, daily activities, routines, and traditions

Objectives

Cross-cultural courses, as part of the general education curriculum, are designed to help students:

- Understand the interdependence of world systems and the ways global inequality affects quality of life and life chances for people in the world

doi:10.1300/5609_13

- Develop increased understanding and appreciation for cultural traditions significantly different from their own and become aware of how people from different cultures perceive the world, interpret reality, and make meaning
- Understand the paradoxes, tensions, and contradictions, as well as consistencies and values in a society significantly different than their own
- Reflect upon their own culture and society from the perspective of another culture
- Develop an appropriate sense of cultural relativism and reduce ethnocentrism
- Gain skills and experience living and working in a culture different from their own

Faculty members may develop additional, more specific educational objectives for their particular course contexts. Often, these are unique to the specific skills or disciplinary knowledge they wish their students to acquire.

Rationale

Increased "globalization" and interdependence amongst different nations worldwide has emphasized the need to assist students in understanding people of other societies (Boyer, 1987). "Closed classrooms" are inadequate in helping students fully understand and resolve issues facing societies today (Kraft, 1992, p. 8). International study opportunities are excellent experiential learning options and are designed to help students understand and develop an appreciation for societies and cultures different from their own (Flack, 1981; Gochenour, 1993; Kraft, 1992; Neff, 1981; Scarce, 1997). In reviewing the impact of international experience on students, Wilson (1993) identified gaining a global perspective via substantive knowledge and perceptual understanding, as well as developing self and relationships through personal growth and interpersonal connections. Such students are also likely to develop an international perspective "in their perceptions of host and home cultures and in their global understanding" (p. 55). By acknowledging the responsibility to adequately prepare future family professionals for cross-cultural competence, greater global perspective, and awareness (Tonkin, 1993), and a better understanding of families in society (National Council on Family Relations, 2004 #1), family science educators need to explore creative ways to help students succeed in a multicultural world (Prather & Lovett-Scott, 2002).

PROCEDURES

Cross-cultural study courses at our undergraduate college are housed within the general education program, are three weeks in duration, have no course prerequisites, serve as an option in fulfilling a portion of the foreign language requirement, and occur during the college's January term or May term. Faculty in any discipline, assuming that the faculty members possess the necessary expertise about the particular culture, can teach these courses. Because they can be taken by students in any major (e.g., family science, English, art, music, engineering), students from a variety of disciplines are presented with the opportunity to learn about families and cultures different from their own. Typically, two faculty members colead these courses and share the responsibility for preparation and planning, travel, and instruction. Twenty-four students need to participate in order for each faculty member to receive three hours of credit toward his or her teaching load for the spring semester. Destinations in these travel-abroad courses are largely dependent upon faculty interest and expertise, but currently include such countries as: the Bahamas, Belize, Brazil, Costa Rica, the Czech Republic, England, Guadeloupe, Guatemala/ Belize, Holland, India, Ireland, Israel, Kenya, Malaysia/Singapore, Mexico, Nepal, Peru, Portugal, Puerto Rico, Scotland, Spain, Trinidad and Tobago, Zambia, and Zimbabwe.

Typical Expectations and Assignments

Given that the cross-cultural course is designed to provide students with sustained contact with people and families of the host culture rather than merely serve as a tour group, cross-cultural leaders are expected to include at least one of three pedagogical options—home stays, ethnographies, and/or service projects—in their courses. Home stays, the most frequently employed attempt at cultural immersion, offer students the opportunity to participate in daily family life for a portion of the three-week trip. Host families are remunerated for housing one to three students for up to one week's duration. During this time, students join the host family in activities of daily living, eating meals with the family, spending time with the children (if there are any), and participating in family-related events.

Ethnographic fieldwork, a second option, is also deemed an acceptable strategy for fostering personal and sustained interaction with individuals in the host culture. Engaging in fieldwork, asking questions, interviewing (Spradley, 1979), and incorporating participant observation methodologies (Laubscher, 1994) are elements of this focus. In this case, students are instructed in the ethnographic method and are asked to write ethnographies or other topical papers on a specific area of interest (e.g., mate selection practices, gender roles, child care, health care systems, work, art, religion, family businesses, care of the aged).

Finally, organizing and participating in service projects in which students and faculty work side by side with those in the host culture is an acceptable option for cross-cultural courses (see Myers-Lipton, 1996). These projects are typically arranged by the faculty member prior to departure and are sensitive to the needs of and opportunities available within the host country. In past cross-culturals, students and faculty have assisted residents with hurricane cleanup, participated in construction or beautification projects, organized recreational or artistic activities for classes of elementary school children, and other such activities. Regardless of which of the three major educational elements (home stay, ethnography, or service) is implemented into the cross-cultural experience, student reflection is deemed a crucial part of the overall experience. Students reflect upon their learning in journals, papers, informal discussions, and group-processing sessions.

Students also learn about families, cultures, and life experiences different from their own through any variety of exercises and assignments particular to a specific cross-cultural destination. Some possibilities include: reading required books (e.g., history books, travel guidebooks, novels, or autobiographies by native authors); sharing in planning, as well as participating in field trips (e.g., schools, factories, historic sites, orphanages, museums, police colleges, day care centers, retirement/old age homes, cathedrals or mosques, theaters) (see McKay & Parson,1986 for helpful guidelines for planning field trips); maintaining a reading journal and/or field notes; and writing papers, including reflective and integrative papers. Projects specifically designed to enhance understanding of family life might include: exploring family traditions and customs or local festivals in the area; examining family-related policies in the host country; interviewing the host family about a series of topics; shadowing professionals who work on behalf of individuals and families; participating in a "scavenger hunt" in a particular community; and attending lectures or presentations provided by local residents/experts on family-related topics.

Numerous sources offer suggestions for faculty and students participating in international study. Hess (1997) provides several methods that students can be taught for facilitating culture learning (e.g., reflection, action-reflection-response technique, values and ethical choices analyses). Many authors address ways in which participants can prepare for *culture shock* (Bochner, 1986; Oberg, 1960), anxiety that is common when people are placed in foreign environments (Guthrie, 1975; Kraft, 1992). Pepin (1993) offers a short guide to designing and conducting experiential exercises, which can help students prepare for what they are about to encounter. Other educators recommend and provide specific exercises to promote self-awareness and intercultural competence (Batchelder, 1993; Fantini & Dant, 1993; Foster, 1994; Gloria, Rieckmann, & Rush, 2000; Gochenour, 1993; Viramontez Anguiano & Harrison, 2002). In addition to numerous other guidelines for successful short-term, study-abroad programs, Henthorne, Miller & Hudson (2001) recommend student research projects in the host country as a particularly effective strategy of initiating interaction between the students and local residents in order to produce a more meaningful and insightful experience. Gaston (1984) introduces a variety of engaging and creative techniques that can enhance intercultural adjustment skills.

Logistical Details

Taking students to another country for three weeks involves an incredible amount of preparatory work. (See checklist of planning responsibilities in the Appendix.) Planning begins more than one year in advance, as specific course proposals are submitted to the General Education Curriculum Committee for approval. Once approved, recruiting for particular cross-cultural courses takes place approximately twelve months prior to departure. Several months of lead time allow the instructors to ascertain that they have a full class and ensures students that space is reserved for them, thus permitting them to begin saving for the additional travel fees. Faculty leaders need to develop a budget that includes such things as airfares, hotel accommodations, ground transportation, and the like.

Selection procedures for determining which students to accept into the course need to be developed. Many leaders personally interview each applicant (those serious enough to have made the required $100 deposit). Questions assessing such things as student flexibility, attitude, academic performance, and ability to get along with others are typically included in the brief interview. Students must provide two references (faculty or curricular educators) who in turn are asked to fill out a reference form. Students are typically informed seven months prior to the date of departure as to whether they have been selected to go. A waiting list of four to five students is maintained in the event that one or more students needs to withdraw from the course.

Once it is determined who will be participating in the course, orientation meetings should include objectives and expectations of the course, travel information (e.g., itinerary, emergency contact numbers for parents, required immunizations, packing lists, travel advisory information, passport acquisition information), introductory and team-building exercises, participant observation methodologies instruction, and orientation to the host country. These meetings can occur sporadically during the month or so prior to departure or the day before leaving for the host country. During these few sessions, we introduce concepts such as ethnocentrism and cultural relativism, review expectations of the course, and present the basics of participant observation and ethnographic methodology.

Institutions may require the observance of certain procedures as well. Faculty leaders should be sure to collect and file institutional liability waiver forms prior to departure, if they are necessary. Faculty will want to obtain student emergency medical information and be aware of any institutional insurance policies or evacuation procedures. Copies of passports and individual plane tickets are also helpful in the event of unforeseen problems (e.g., lost or stolen passport, medical emergency). A first-aid kit, provided by the university health center, is crucial and should include medications and health supplies most likely to be needed in the country of destination. It is also generally a good idea to provide a list of participants and a copy of the itinerary to both the academic office at the university and the United States Embassy in the host country prior to departure. A phone directory of important personal contacts and emergency numbers in the host country should be developed and taken along as well.

Faculty coleaders are also responsible for making all transportation (e.g., airline tickets, car/van rentals) and housing (e.g., hotels and home stays) arrangements. Some faculty secure home stays based on personal contacts with residents of the host country or work through churches, tourist bureaus, or other reputable agencies. We have found that items (e.g., pens, umbrellas, miniflashlights, or canvas bags with the college logo) purchased for the trip serve as great gifts for guest speakers, host families, bus drivers, and other helpful people in the host country.

Once in the host country, faculty leaders are busy coordinating daily schedules of transportation, instruction, field trips, meals, and the like. The group meets regularly to discuss readings, take quizzes, process their experiences, and have fun. Faculty members serve as guides or coaches in modeling cultural sensitivity, respect, and adventurousness. They are available to assist the students with independent research projects, course assignments, or the planning of individual or class excursions. During the home-stay portion of the trip, it is ideal if the faculty members also stay in a home. Wherever housed, however, students should be informed as to how they can reach the faculty members, should the need arise.

Papers and other projects are often not due until a week or so after returning home. Several weeks after returning to campus, it is also nice to host a gathering where students can receive refunds of excess money, share their photos of the trip, and reminisce about and further process their experience.

CASE EXAMPLE: BAHAMAS CROSS-CULTURAL TRIP

The following is an example of a Bahamas cross-cultural trip, co-led by Hamon. Though students from any discipline are eligible to participate in this course, students within the Department of Human Development and Family Science (HDFS) are especially encouraged to be involved. The course is designed to provide students with the opportunity to examine and explore Bahamian history and culture through a variety of media, including books, seminars and lectures, guest speakers, fieldwork, and visits to major cultural sites, with particular attention to Bahamian families. This course requires students to spend a minimum of fifty contact hours with Bahamian individuals and families and complete an ethnography on some aspect of Bahamian culture. HDFS students typically select topics such as mate selection, Bahamian food, community festivals, childrens' play, child rearing, couple relationships, and roles for and care of the aged. In addition, students complete several reading assignments, maintain a journal of personal reflections, and, in small groups, plan a field trip for the class. Student grades are determined based on performance on exams which cover reading assignments, quality of ethnography, and participation and level of engagement in the experience.

ASSESSMENT/EVALUATION

The results of a survey of students in a cross-cultural course in January 2004 (Philadelphia, Zambia, England; 2004) indicates the value of these courses to the undergraduate experience. With a survey response rate of 90 percent, results suggested that: the majority (94.9 percent) of students developed a greater interest in learning about other cultures; most (89.7 percent) felt that the experience prepared them to communicate with people who are ethnically, linguistically, and culturally different; and 96.2 percent increased their appreciation for cultural traditions different from their own. Overall, students developed a greater acceptance of cultural diversity and reported learning a great deal about history, social structure, institutions, and many other aspects of culture when participating in these courses. In addition, many students indicated religious benefits, including spiritual growth (88.6 percent).

Formal course evaluations completed by student participants in the most recent Bahamas cross-cultural trip (January 2001) offered instructive feedback. On measures of overall teaching effectiveness for this course, students indicated that they developed "more positive feelings toward this area of study" (score of 3.9 on a 5-point scale). Students also indicated that the course met the following objectives: gaining factual knowledge, improving team skills, increasing an understanding and appreciation of intellectual and cultural activities, developing oral and written communication skills, using resources to answer questions, and analyzing/evaluating ideas. In open-ended responses, students expressed appreciation for the freedom and trust the faculty members demonstrated for participants and felt that there was an appropriate balance between planned activities and free time. Suggestions for improvement mainly included the desire to participate in more field trips and activities with local schools and churches and more adequate preparation prior to departure. One student also suggested a longer trip with more time to interact with Bahamian hosts.

CONCLUSION

International cross-cultural encounters continue to be an excellent means of exposing students to cultural and family diversity. Living in a strange environment, even for a short period of time, can provide a life-changing experience for young adults. Being confronted by living standards different from one's own, recognizing the centrality of language (both verbal and nonverbal) in understanding others, feeling self-conscious for being and looking different, facing one's own ethnocentricity, and observing similarities and differences in family life are just some of the ways in which cross-culturals can have an impact on student thinking, emotions, and values.

A combination of factors seems to make for successful international educational encounters. First, experienced faculty leaders are important. Knowledge of the host country, established contacts with resource people and host families, and experience with what works are all important in helping the trip to run smoothly. Educators have the dual responsibility of providing cognitive knowledge as well as introducing the learners to a variety of social experiences (Rosenheck, 1988). Faculty members need to be discriminating about what skills or knowledge is critical for students prior to departure (e.g., participant observation methodology, language, information about others in travel group) and what instruction can be accomplished in the host country. Faculty members should remain cognizant of critical educational goals and objectives and be creative in trying to attain them.

Second, some type of sustained and significant interaction with people in the host country is imperative for real learning to take place (Abrams, 1979) and distinguishes this cultural encounter from a traveling tour group. Although ethnographic research and service options are useful teaching strategies, home stays seem to be a particularly effective means for cultural immersion. Home stays give students the opportunity to interact with individuals who can be key informants about the host culture (Laubscher, 1994). For the family science student, they also provide the opportunity to observe and participate in the internal workings of a foreign family.

Third, students need to be kept well-informed about expectations and itinerary, as well as be encouraged to be flexible, adaptable, and adventurous. Traveling in a group, living closely with people for an extended period of time, experiencing the normal fatigue of full itineraries, culture shock, and being in unfamiliar surroundings pose challenges to the most agreeable personalities at times. Special attention may need to be devoted to the maintenance of positive group dynamics.

Fourth, in addition to meeting disciplinary/educational objectives, the cross-cultural course has the ability to help students achieve personal milestones in their own developmental process. Flexibility in itinerary and assignments that allows students to shape their own learning experiences offers numerous personal benefits. Students given an opportunity to plan portions of their own itinerary feel a sense of accomplishment and independence unlike those participating in highly structured courses.

Finally, opportunities for academic, as well as personal reflection facilitate learning about other cultures and the families which are located within them. Students need to be able to test their cultural understanding by asking questions and sharing insights with their peers, professors, and host families. Reflection is an avenue for students to incorporate their observations with information they gain from textbook learning (Laubscher, 1994). Reflection gives students the opportunity to integrate their previous classroom knowledge with their cross-cultural course and gain a more complex understanding of their experience. Fostering various avenues and contexts for this reflective process is an important responsibility of the faculty leader.

Cross-cultural courses, particularly those specifically designed to teach about families, provide an excellent option for exposing students to one or more of the ten "substance areas" for the National Council on Family Relations' Certified Family Life Education Program (Powell & Cassidy, 2001). International contexts are ideal for creatively teaching the families in society substance area. Such courses certainly help students to better understand "lifestyles of families in various societies around the world" (Powell & Cassidy, 2001, p. 231), exposing them to how families around the globe interface with other institutions (i.e., schools, government, religious institutions, and businesses/employers). Depending upon the types of assignments and readings employed, other substance areas could easily be addressed as well. For instance, the home-stay experience facilitates firsthand observations of internal dynamics of families. Journal entries and survey responses suggest that students are quite capable of making observations about "how family members relate to each other" (Powell & Cassidy, 2001, p. 231), how families communicate, handle stress and conflict, establish patterns of interaction, and care for their members. At the same time, students engaging in ethnographic projects that examine housing and the use of space, teenage sexual behavior, parenting practices, or family communication skills could easily gain competence in substance areas of family resource management, human sexuality, parent education and guidance, and interpersonal relationships, respectively. Well-planned, cross-cultural courses, with carefully delineated educational objectives and thoughtfully designed activities and projects, offer tremendous learning opportunities for family science students and faculty.

APPENDIX: CROSS-CULTURAL COURSE CHECKLIST

1. Select colleague as coleader
2. Submit course proposal to appropriate college committee
3. Develop budget
4. Advertise cross-cultural course; include approximate cost
5. Collect applications/deposits
6. Interview applicants
7. Inform students selected
8. Develop syllabus, including itinerary
9. Create packing list for students
10. Create phone directory of emergency contacts
11. Hold orientation meetings for students
    a. Engage in introductory and team-building exercises
    b. Provide orientation information on the host country
    c. Offer ethnographic instruction
    d. Provide journal guidelines
    e. Distribute syllabus, itinerary, and phone directory of emergency contacts
    f. Hand out packing list for students
    g. Provide an estimated amount of money/traveler's checks needed for the trip

       h. Inform students of required immunizations
       i. Give passport acquisition information
       j. Collect completed liability waiver forms, medical information, and copies of passports
12. Develop packing list for faculty, include:
       a. First-aid kit
       b. Gifts for hosts
       c. Copies of all passports/tickets
       d. Phone/address directory of contacts
13. Purchase airline tickets
14. Reserve housing
15. Reserve cars/ground/water transportation
16. Organize home stays
17. Order/purchase thank-you gifts (hosts, speakers)
18. Purchase travelers' checks/secure college credit card
19. Order books
20. Students purchase books
21. Create quizzes/study guides
22. Remain abreast of travel advisories
23. Contact United States Embassy and provide list of students/leaders' names and itinerary
24. Grade papers/journals
25. Schedule and plan picture party/reunion after return
26. Academic follow up for students

REFERENCES

Abrams, I. (1979). The impact of Antioch education through experience abroad. *Alternative Higher Education, 3,* 176-187.

Batchelder, D. (1993). Preparation for cross-cultural experience. In T. Gochenour (Ed.), *Beyond experience* (Second edition) (pp. 59-71). Yarmouth, ME: World Learning.

Bochner, S. (1986). Coping with unfamiliar cultures: Adjustment or culture learning? *Australian Journal of Psychology, 38,* 347-358.

Boyer, E.L. (1987*). College: The undergraduate experience in America.* New York: Harper & Row.

Fantini, A.E. & Dant, W.P. (1993). Language and intercultural orientation: A process approach. In T. Gochenour (Ed.), *Beyond experience* (Second edition) (pp. 79-96). Yarmouth, ME: World Learning.

Flack, M.J. (1981). Experiential learning in transnational contexts. *New Directions for Experiential Learning, 11,* 11-19.

Foster, J. (1994). Intercultural competence through experience based training. In *Experiential education: A critical resource for the 21st century. Proceedings Manual of the Annual International Conference of the Association for Experiential Education, 22,* 130-133.

Gaston, J. (1984). *Cultural awareness teaching techniques.* Brattleboro, VT: Pro Lingua Associates.

Gloria, A.M., Rieckmann, T.R., & Rush, J.D. (2000). Issues and recommendations for teaching an ethnic/culture-based course. *Teaching Psychology, 27,* 102-107.

Gochenour, T. (Ed.). (1993). Beyond experience (Second edition). Yarmouth, ME: World Learning.

Guthrie, G.M. (1975). A behavioral analysis of culture learning. In R.W. Brislin, S. Bochner, & W.J. Lonner (Eds.), *Cross-cultural perspectives on learning* (pp. 95-115). New York: Sage.

Henthorne, T.L., Miller, M.M., & Hudson, T.W. (2001). Building and positioning successful study-abroad programs: A "hands-on" approach. *Journal of Teaching in International Business, 12,* 49-62.

Hess, J.D. (1997). *Studying abroad/learning abroad.* Yarmouth, ME: Intercultural Press.

Kraft, R.J. (1992). Closed classrooms, high mountains and strange lands: An inquiry into culture and caring. *The Journal of Experiential Education, 15,* 8-15.

Laubscher, M.R. (1994). *Encounters with difference: Student perceptions of the role of out-of-class experiences in education abroad.* Westport, CT: Greenwood.

McKay, I.A. & Parson, H.E. (1986). *The successful field trip.* Dubuque, IA: Kendall/Hunt.

Myers-Lipton, S.J. (1996). Effect of service-learning on college students' attitudes toward international understanding. *Journal of College Student Development, 37,* 659-667.

National Council on Family Relations. (2004). *"Family Life Education Substance Areas."* Retrieved May 4, 2004, from http://www.ncfr.org/pdf/FLE_Substance_Areas.pdf.

Neff, C.B. (Ed.). (1981). *New directions for experiential learning: Cross-cultural learning.* San Francisco, CA: Jossey-Bass.

Oberg, K. (1960). Culture shock: Adjustment to new cultural environments. *Practical Anthropology, 7,* 177-182.

Pepin, C. (1993). A short guide to designing and conducting an experiential exercise. In T. Gochenour (Ed.), *Beyond experience* (Second edition) (pp. 73-77). Yarmouth, ME: World Learning.

Powell, L.H. & Cassidy, D. (2001). *Family life education: An introduction.* Mountain View, CA: Mayfield.

Prather, F. & Lovett-Scott, M. (2002). How demographic destinies affect teaching and learning: Innovative strategies for the 21st century educator. *The Delta Kappa Gamma Bulletin, 68,* 5-14.

Rosenheck, D. (1988). Field trips abroad. *Social Education, 52,* 344-346.

Scarce, R. (1997). Field trips as short-term experiential education. *Teaching Sociology, 25,* 219-226.

Spradley, J.P. (1979). *The ethnographic interview.* Orlando, FL: Holt, Rinehart & Winston.

Tonkin, H. (1993). Service, values, and a liberal education. *Action reflection* (pp. 1-3). New York: Partnership for Service Learning.

Viramontez Anguiano, R.P. & Harrison, S.M. (2002). Teaching cultural diversity to college students majoring in helping professions: The use of the eco-strengths perspective. *College Student Journal, 36,* 152-156.

Wilson, A.H. (1993). The meaning of international experience for schools. Westport, CT: Praeger.

Index

Page numbers followed by the letter "f" indicate figures; those followed by "t" indicate tables.

Order a copy of this book with this form or online at:
http://www.haworthpress.com/store/product.asp?sku=5609

INTERNATIONAL FAMILY STUDIES
Developing Curricula and Teaching Tools

_____in hardbound at $44.95 (ISBN-13: 978-0-7890-2923-2; ISBN-10: 0-7890-2923-5)

_____in softbound at $34.95 (ISBN-13: 978-0-7890-2924-9; ISBN-10: 0-7890-2924-3)

Or order online and use special offer code HEC25 in the shopping cart.

COST OF BOOKS_____

☐ **BILL ME LATER:** (Bill-me option is good on US/Canada/Mexico orders only; not good to jobbers, wholesalers, or subscription agencies.)

☐ Check here if billing address is different from shipping address and attach purchase order and billing address information.

POSTAGE & HANDLING_____
(US: $4.00 for first book & $1.50 for each additional book)
(Outside US: $5.00 for first book & $2.00 for each additional book)

Signature_____

SUBTOTAL_____

☐ **PAYMENT ENCLOSED:** $_____

IN CANADA: ADD 7% GST_____

☐ **PLEASE CHARGE TO MY CREDIT CARD.**

STATE TAX_____
(NJ, NY, OH, MN, CA, IL, IN, PA, & SD residents, add appropriate local sales tax)

☐ Visa ☐ MasterCard ☐ AmEx ☐ Discover
☐ Diner's Club ☐ Eurocard ☐ JCB

Account # _____

FINAL TOTAL_____
(If paying in Canadian funds, convert using the current exchange rate, UNESCO coupons welcome)

Exp. Date_____

Signature_____

Prices in US dollars and subject to change without notice.

NAME_____

INSTITUTION_____

ADDRESS_____

CITY_____

STATE/ZIP_____

COUNTRY_____ COUNTY (NY residents only)_____

TEL_____ FAX_____

E-MAIL_____

May we use your e-mail address for confirmations and other types of information? ☐ Yes ☐ No We appreciate receiving your e-mail address and fax number. Haworth would like to e-mail or fax special discount offers to you, as a preferred customer. **We will never share, rent, or exchange your e-mail address or fax number.** We regard such actions as an invasion of your privacy.

Order From Your Local Bookstore or Directly From
The Haworth Press, Inc.
10 Alice Street, Binghamton, New York 13904-1580 • USA
TELEPHONE: 1-800-HAWORTH (1-800-429-6784) / Outside US/Canada: (607) 722-5857
FAX: 1-800-895-0582 / Outside US/Canada: (607) 771-0012
E-mail to: orders@haworthpress.com

For orders outside US and Canada, you may wish to order through your local sales representative, distributor, or bookseller.
For information, see http://haworthpress.com/distributors

(Discounts are available for individual orders in US and Canada only, not booksellers/distributors.)

PLEASE PHOTOCOPY THIS FORM FOR YOUR PERSONAL USE.
http://www.HaworthPress.com   BOF06